AN INTRODUCTION TO METAPHYSICS

MARTIN HEIDEGGER was born in 1889 at Messkirch in Baden, Germany. He attended the university at nearby Freiburg and there met Edmund Husserl whose *phenomenology* was to have a marked influence on Heidegger's thought. In 1915 he became Privatdocent at the University of Freiburg, and in 1923 professor of philosophy at Marburg. While at Marburg, Heidegger published *Sein und Zeit* (1927) (*Being and Time*) which, though not completed, nevertheless stands as his masterwork. In 1929 Heidegger succeeded Husserl to the Chair of Philosophy at Freiburg, and four years later, when the National Socialists were in power, he was appointed Rector of the university, a post which he resigned in 1935. Ten years after this, following Germany's surrender in the Second World War, Heidegger was dismissed from his Chair of Philosophy because of alleged Nazi sympathies. He thereupon retired to a life of seclusion near Freiburg. AN INTRODUCTION TO METAPHYSICS made its first printed appearance, in German (*Einführung in die Metaphysik*), in 1953, although the essential material had been presented eighteen years before in one of his university lectures.

AN INTRODUCTION
TO METAPHYSICS

Martin Heidegger

Translated by Ralph Manheim

Anchor Books
Doubleday & Company, Inc.
Garden City, New York
1961

TYPOGRAPHY BY SUSAN SIEN

CONTENTS

TRANSLATOR'S NOTE

For Heidegger the whole history of human thought and existence has been dominated and characterized by man's understanding of being; the disorientation of modern thought and existence is rooted in "forgetfulness of being." In an *Introduction to Metaphysics* he accordingly investigates the meaning of being and the history of man's understanding of being.

He finds this history and this meaning recorded in philosophy, poetry, and above all in the language that underlies them both. ". . . words and language," he writes, (p. 11) "are not wrappings . . . for . . . those who write and speak. It is in words and language that things first come into being and are." And further on: (p. 42) ". . . the destroyed relation to being as such is the actual reason for the general misrelation to language." This explains why so much of the present book is taken up with the origin and vicissitudes of words. It also accounts in large part for Heidegger's style and the difficulty of translating him. Attaching the importance he does to words, he uses them very carefully, taking account of their "weights" and overtones. These of course vary from language to language.

Every writer of any character is deeply involved in his own language. But this is true of Heidegger in a special sense, "For along with German the Greek language is (in regard to its possibilities for thought) at once the most powerful and most spiritual of all languages" (p. 47). And it is perfectly true that no other language has been moulded to the same degree as German by idealistic philosophy. A translator sometimes asks himself: How would the author have said this in my language? Here too this method has its application, for luckily English and German have a good deal in common. But it also has its limits, because if Heidegger had been at home in English—this less "spiritual" language—he would have written (and thought) differently. It does little good to ask how he would have said "in-sich-aus-sich-hinausstehen" in my language. And the same problem arises when a German word (such as "Not," p. 136 f., or "Fug," p. 134) has overtones that cannot be suggested by any English word. In such cases it often seems necessary to choose between fluency and meaning. My choice has always been to attempt, by every means I could find, to convey the meaning. Heidegger himself makes this choice. He is a very eloquent writer but he does not hesitate to write in harsh, broken periods when his meaning demands it. He is often strange in German and he will often be strange in English, though not always in the same places.

This is a book about "Sein" in its relation to "Seiendes" and "Dasein." The English word "being" is an almost satisfactory equivalent for "Sein." I say "almost," because "Sein" is an infinitive while "being" is of participial origin, and this creates complications in connection with Heidegger's grammatical analyses. As to "seiend," it is a philosophical invention, a word "alien to everyday speech" (p. 64). From the standpoint both of style and of meaning it has seemed to me essential to render "seiend" by the same word throughout, a word that is part of the verb "to be" and "alien to everyday speech." But there is no such word in English. "Existent" has often been used. There are two objections: 1) it does not derive from the verb "to be"; 2) it means something else in Heidegger. Another solution has been to render "Das Seiende" as "What is" and "ein Seiendes" and "die Seienden" respectively as "a being" and "beings." Though I have used "what is" in one or two places where it seemed eminently to fit, I have in the main discarded these solutions. For one thing, the constant use of two different words for this key term seems to obscure Heidegger's thought. For another, I should have been driven to such turns of phrase as "the being that belongs to every being," "the troublesome circumstance that being is not a being," "a copy as it were of the experienced being." In the last it is not even immediately clear which kind of being is meant.

I have therefore taken the liberty to coin a word: "essent," "essents," "the essent," based on the fiction that *essens, essentis* is the present participle of *sum*. I hope the bad Latin is not too strong an objection to my word.

"Dasein" raises a different kind of problem. It is an everyday German word meaning "existence." But Heidegger breaks it down into its components, "being" and "there," and gives it a very particular meaning (see note p. 8). I have rendered it throughout as "being-there," because not only Heidegger's "Da-sein" but his "Dasein" as well has a special definition and dignity that are lacking in the colorless "existence."

A word must be said about Heidegger's translations from the Greek, which differ radically from other translations of the same texts. Heidegger's translations are based on his investigations of Greek words and Greek thought. Since his interpretations of words and thought are very different from the traditional ones, it is only natural that his translations should be different from traditional translations. What I have rendered is Heidegger's versions and not the Greek originals.

As Heidegger explains in his Preface, he himself has used parentheses and square brackets in the text. These remain unchanged in the translation. For the insertions I myself have been obliged to make I have used angle brackets: ⟨ . . .⟩. These usually enclose German words when I was unable to carry a play on words or roots into the translation. Sometimes they contain brief explanatory remarks.

I am indebted for help and advice to Norbert Guterman, Joseph Frank, John Wild of Harvard University, Charles Hendel of Yale University, and Jean Wahl of the Sorbonne whose commentary on the present work, *Vers la fin de l'ontologie*, Paris, 1956, I consulted freely.

Prefatory Note to the German Edition of 1953

The present volume contains the fully reworked text of the lecture bearing the same title that I delivered at the University of Freiburg in Breisgau in the summer semester of 1935.

There is a difference between the spoken and the written word.

I have made *no change in the content,* but as a help to the reader I have broken up long sentences, introduced connectives, deleted repetitions, remedied oversights, and rectified imprecisions.

Matter in parentheses was written while I was reworking the text. The square brackets contain remarks added in the ensuing years.

In order to understand fully in what sense and for what reason the term "metaphysics" is included in the title, the reader must first have participated in the development of the lecture.

AN INTRODUCTION TO METAPHYSICS

THE FUNDAMENTAL QUESTION OF METAPHYSICS

Why are there essents* rather than nothing? That is the question. Clearly it is no ordinary question. "Why are there essents, why is there anything at all, rather than nothing?"—obviously this is the first of all questions, though not in a chronological sense. Individuals and peoples ask a good many questions in the course of their historical passage through time. They examine, explore, and test a good many things before they run into the question "Why are there essents rather than nothing?" Many men never encounter this question, if by encounter we mean not merely to hear and read about it as an interrogative formulation but to ask the question, that is, to bring it about, to raise it, to feel its inevitability.

And yet each of us is grazed at least once, perhaps more than once, by the hidden power of this question, even if he is not aware of what is happening to him. The question looms in moments of great despair, when things tend to lose all their weight and all meaning becomes obscured. Perhaps it will strike but once like a muffled bell that rings into our life and gradually dies away. It is present in moments of rejoicing, when all the things around us are transfigured and seem to be there for the first time, as if it might be easier to think they are not than to understand that they are and are as they are. The question is upon us in boredom, when we are equally removed from despair and joy, and everything about us seems

* "Essents" = "existents," "things that are." See Translator's Note, p. xi.

so hopelessly commonplace that we no longer care whether anything is or is not—and with this the question "Why are there essents rather than nothing?" is evoked in a particular form.

But this question may be asked expressly, or, unrecognized as a question, it may merely pass through our lives like a brief gust of wind; it may press hard upon us, or, under one pretext or another, we may thrust it away from us and silence it. In any case it is never the question that we ask first in point of time.

But it is the first question in another sense—in regard to rank. This may be clarified in three ways. The question "Why are there essents rather than nothing?" is first in rank for us first because it is the most far reaching, second because it is the deepest, and finally because it is the most fundamental of all questions.

It is the widest of all questions. It confines itself to no particular essent of whatever kind. The question takes in everything, and this means not only everything that is present in the broadest sense but also everything that ever was or will be. The range of this question finds its limit only in nothing, in that which simply is not and never was. Everything that is not nothing is covered by this question, and ultimately even nothing itself; not because it is *something*, since after all we speak of it, but because it *is* nothing. Our question reaches out so far that we can never go further. We do not inquire into this and that, or into each essent in turn, but from the very outset into the essent as a whole, or, as we say for reasons to be discussed below: into the essent as such in its entirety.

This broadest of questions is also the deepest: Why are there essents . . . ? Why, that is to say, on what ground? from what source does the essent derive? on what ground does it stand? The question is not concerned with particulars, with what essents are and of what nature at any time, here and there, with how they can be changed, what they can be used for, and so on. The question aims at the ground of what is insofar as it is. To seek the ground is to try to get to the bottom; what is put in question is thus related to the ground. However, since the question is a question, it remains to be seen whether the ground arrived at is really a ground, that is, whether it provides a foundation; whether it is a primal ground ⟨ Ur-grund ⟩; or whether it fails to provide a foundation and is an abyss ⟨ Ab-grund ⟩; or whether the ground is neither one nor the other but presents only a perhaps necessary appearance of foundation—in other words, it is a nonground ⟨ Un-grund ⟩. Be that as it may, the ground in question must account for the being of the essent as such. This question "why" does not look for causes that are of the same kind and on the same level as the essent itself. This "why" does not move on any one plane but penetrates to the "underlying" ⟨ "zu-grunde" liegend ⟩ realms and indeed to the very last of them, to the limit; turning away from the surface, from all shallowness, it strives toward the depths; this broadest of all questions is also the deepest.

Finally, this broadest and deepest question is also the most fundamental. What do we mean by this? If we take the question in its full scope, namely the essent as such in its entirety, it readily follows that in asking this question we keep our distance from every particular and individual essent, from every this and that. For we mean the essent as a whole, without any special preference. Still, it is noteworthy that in this questioning *one* kind of essent persists in coming to the fore, namely the men who ask the question. But the question should not concern itself with any particular essent. In the spirit of its unrestricted scope, all essents are of equal value. An elephant in an Indian jungle "is" just as much as some chemical combustion process at work on the planet Mars, and so on.

Accordingly, if our question "Why are there essents rather than nothing?" is taken in its fullest sense, we must avoid singling out any special, particular essent, including man. For what indeed is man? Consider the earth within the endless darkness of space in the universe. By way of comparison it is a tiny grain of sand; between it and the next grain of its own size there extends a mile or more of emptiness; on the surface of this grain of sand there lives a crawling, bewildered swarm of supposedly intelligent animals, who for a moment have discovered knowledge.* And what is the temporal exten-

---

* Cf. Nietzsche, *Über Wahrheit und Lüge im aussermoralischen Sinne.* 1873 *Nachlass.*

sion of a human life amid all the millions of years? Scarcely a move of the second hand, a breath. Within the essent as a whole there is no legitimate ground for singling out this essent which is called mankind and to which we ourselves happen to belong.

But whenever the essent as a whole enters into this question, a privileged, unique relation arises between it and the act of questioning. For through this questioning the essent as a whole is for the first time opened up *as such* with a view to its possible ground, and in the act of questioning it is kept open. In relation to the essent as such in its entirety the asking of the question is not just any occurrence within the realm of the essent, like the falling of raindrops for example. The question "why" may be said to confront the essent as a whole, to break out of it, though never completely. But that is exactly why the act of questioning is privileged. Because it confronts the essent as a whole, but does not break loose from it, the content of the question reacts upon the questioning itself. Why the why? What is the ground of this question "why" which presumes to ask after the ground of the essent as a whole? Is the ground asked for in *this* why not merely a foreground—which would imply that the sought-for ground is again an essent? Does not the "first" question nevertheless come first in view of the intrinsic rank of the question of being and its modulations?

To be sure, the things in the world, the essents, are in no way affected by our asking of the question "Why are there essents rather than nothing?" Whether we ask it or not, the planets move in their orbits, the sap of life flows through plant and animal.

But *if* this question is asked and if the act of questioning is really carried out, the content and the object of the question react inevitably on the act of questioning. Accordingly this questioning is not just any occurrence but a privileged happening that we call an *event*.

This question and all the questions immediately rooted in it, the questions in which this one question unfolds—this question "why" is incommensurable with any other. It encounters the search for its own why. At first sight the question "Why the why?" looks like a frivolous repetition ad infinitum of the same interrogative formulation, like an empty and unwarranted brooding over words. Yes, beyond a doubt, that is how it looks. The question is only whether we wish to be taken in by this superficial look and so regard the whole matter as settled, or whether we are capable of finding a significant event in this recoil of the question "why" upon itself.

But if we decline to be taken in by surface appearances we shall see that this question "why," this question as to the essent as such in its entirety, goes beyond any mere playing with words, provided we possess sufficient intellectual energy to make the question actually recoil into its "why"—for it will not do so of its own accord. In so doing we find out that this privileged question "why" has its ground in a leap through which man thrusts away all the previous security, whether real or imagined, of his life. The question is asked only in this leap; it *is* the leap; without it there is no asking. What "leap" means here will be elucidated later. Our questioning is not yet the leap; for this it must undergo a transformation; it still stands perplexed in the face of the essent. Here it may suffice to say that the leap in this questioning opens up its own source—with this leap the question arrives at its own ground. We call such a leap, which opens up its own source, the original source or origin ⟨ Ur-sprung ⟩, the finding of one's own ground. It is because the question "Why are there essents rather than nothing?" breaks open the ground for all authentic questions and is thus at the origin ⟨ Ursprung ⟩ of them all that we must recognize it as the most fundamental of all questions.

It is the most fundamental of questions because it is the broadest and deepest, and conversely.

In this threefold sense the question is the first in rank—first, that is, in the order of questioning within the domain which this first question opens, defining its scope and thus founding it. Our question is the *question* of all authentic questions, i.e. of all self-questioning questions, and whether consciously or not it is necessarily implicit in every question. No questioning and accordingly no single scientific "problem" can be fully intelligible if it does not include, i.e. ask, the question of all questions. Let us be clear about this from the start: it can never be objectively determined whether anyone, whether we, really ask this question, that is whether we make the leap, or never get beyond a verbal formula. In a historical setting that does not recognize questioning as a fundamental human force, the question immediately loses its rank.

Anyone for whom the Bible is divine revelation and truth has the answer to the question "Why are there essents rather than nothing?" even before it is asked: everything that is, except God himself, has been created by Him. God himself, the increate creator, "is." One who holds to such faith can in a way participate in the asking of our question, but he cannot really question without ceasing to be a believer and taking all the consequences of such a step. He will only be able to act "as if" . . . On the other hand a faith that does not perpetually expose itself to the possibility of unfaith is no faith but merely a convenience: the believer simply makes up his mind to adhere to the traditional doctrine. This is neither faith nor questioning, but the indifference of those who can busy themselves with everything, sometimes even displaying a keen interest in faith as well as questioning.

What we have said about security in faith as one position in regard to the truth does not imply that the biblical "In the beginning God created heaven and earth" is an answer to our question. Quite aside from whether these words from the Bible are true or false for faith, they can supply no answer to our question because they are in no way related to it. Indeed, they cannot even be brought into relation with our question. From the standpoint of faith our question is "foolishness."

Philosophy is this very foolishness. A "Christian philosophy" is a round square and a misunderstanding. There is, to be sure, a thinking and questioning elaboration of the world of Christian experience, i.e. of faith. That is theology. Only epochs which no longer fully believe in the true greatness of the task of theology arrive at the disastrous notion that philosophy can help to provide a refurbished theology if not a substitute for theology, which will satisfy the needs and tastes of the time. For the original Christian faith philosophy is foolishness. To philosophize is to ask "Why are there essents rather than nothing?" Really to ask the question signifies: a daring attempt to fathom this unfathomable question by disclosing what it summons us to ask, to push our questioning to the very end. Where such an attempt occurs there is philosophy.

It would not serve our purpose to begin our discussion with a detailed report on philosophy. But there are a few things that all must know who wish to concern themselves with philosophy. They can be briefly stated.

All essential philosophical questioning is necessarily untimely. This is so because philosophy is always projected far in advance of its time, or because it connects the present with its antecedent, with what *initially* was. Philosophy always remains a knowledge which not only cannot be adjusted to a given epoch but on the contrary imposes its measure upon its epoch.

Philosophy is essentially untimely because it is one of those few things that can never find an immediate echo in the present. When such an echo seems to occur, when a philosophy becomes fashionable, either it is no real philosophy or it has been misinterpreted and misused for ephemeral and extraneous purposes.

Accordingly, philosophy cannot be directly learned like manual and technical skills; it cannot be directly applied, or judged by its usefulness in the manner of economic or other professional knowledge.

But what is useless can still be a force, perhaps the only real force. What has no immediate echo in everyday life can be intimately bound up with a nation's profound historical development, and can even anticipate it. What is untimely will have its own times. This is true of philosophy. Consequently there is no way of determining once and for all what the task of philosophy is, and accordingly what must be expected of it. Every stage and every beginning of its development bears within it its own law. All that can be said is what philosophy cannot be and cannot accomplish.

A question has been stated: "Why are there essents rather than nothing?" We have claimed first place for this question and explained in what sense it is regarded as first.

We have not even begun to ask the question itself, but have digressed into a discussion about it. Such a digression is indispensable. For this question has nothing in common with our habitual concerns. There is no way of familiarizing ourselves with this question by a gradual transition from the things to

which we are accustomed. Hence it must, as it were, be sin-
gled out in advance, presented. Yet in introducing the question and speaking of it, we must not postpone, let alone forget,
the questioning itself.

Here then let us conclude our preliminary remarks.

Every essential form of spiritual life is marked by ambiguity.
The less commensurate it is with other forms, the more it is
misinterpreted.

Philosophy is one of the few autonomous creative possibilities and at times necessities of man's historical being-
there.* The current misinterpretations of philosophy, all of
which have some truth about them, are legion. Here we shall
mention only two, which are important because of the light
they throw on the present and future situation of philosophy.
The first misinterpretation asks too much of philosophy. The
second distorts its function.

Roughly speaking, philosophy always aims at the first and
last grounds of the essent, with particular emphasis on man
himself and on the meaning and goals of human being-there.
This might suggest that philosophy can and must provide a
foundation on which a nation will build its historical life and
culture. But this is beyond the power of philosophy. As a rule
such excessive demands take the form of a belittling of philosophy. It is said, for example: Because metaphysics did nothing to pave the way for the revolution it should be rejected.
This is no cleverer than saying that because the carpenter's
bench is useless for flying it should be abolished. Philosophy
can never *directly* supply the energies and create the oppor-
tunities and methods that bring about a historical change; for
one thing, because philosophy is always the concern of the
few. Which few? The creators, those who initiate profound

---

* The word "Dasein" is ordinarily translated as "existence." It
is used in "normal," popular discourse. But Heidegger breaks it
into its components "Da" "there" and "Sein" "being," and puts his
own definition on it. In general he means man's conscious, historical
existence in the world, which is always projected into a there beyond its here. The German word Dasein has often been carried
over into translations; the English strikes me as preferable. For
further remarks on "being-there" see the bracketed passage on
pp. 23–4. R.M.

transformations. It spreads only indirectly, by devious paths that can never be laid out in advance, until at last, at some future date, it sinks to the level of a commonplace; but by then it has long been forgotten as original philosophy.

What philosophy essentially can and must be is this: a thinking that breaks the paths and opens the perspectives of the knowledge that sets the norms and hierarchies, of the knowledge in which and by which a people fulfills itself historically and culturally, the knowledge that kindles and necessitates all inquiries and thereby threatens all values.

The second misinterpretation involves a distortion of the function of philosophy. Even if philosophy can provide no foundation for a culture, the argument goes, it is nevertheless a cultural force, whether because it gives us an over-all, systematic view of what is, supplying a useful chart by which we may find our way amid the various possible things and realms of things, or because it relieves the sciences of their work by reflecting on their premises, basic concepts, and principles. Philosophy is expected to promote and even to accelerate—to make easier as it were—the practical and technical business of culture.

But—it is in the very nature of philosophy never to make things easier but only more difficult. And this not merely because its language strikes the everyday understanding as strange if not insane. Rather, it is the authentic function of philosophy to challenge historical being-there and hence, in the last analysis, being pure and simple. It restores to things, to the essents, their weight (being). How so? Because the challenge is one of the essential prerequisites for the birth of all greatness, and in speaking of greatness we are referring primarily to the works and destinies of nations. We can speak of historical destiny only where an authentic knowledge of things dominates man's being-there. And it is philosophy that opens up the paths and perspectives of such knowledge.

The misinterpretations with which philosophy is perpetually beset are promoted most of all by people of our kind, that is, by professors of philosophy. It is our customary business—which may be said to be justified and even useful—to transmit a certain knowledge of the philosophy of the past, as part of a general education. Many people suppose that this is philosophy itself, whereas at best it is the technique of philosophy.

In correcting these two misinterpretations I cannot hope to give you at one stroke a clear conception of philosophy. But I do hope that you will be on your guard when the most current judgments and even supposed observations assail you unawares. Such judgments are often disarming, precisely because they seem so natural. You hear remarks such as "Philosophy leads to nothing," "You can't do anything with philosophy," and readily imagine that they confirm an experience of your own. There is no denying the soundness of these two phrases, particularly common among scientists and teachers of science. Any attempt to refute them by proving that after all it does "lead to something" merely strengthens the prevailing misinterpretation to the effect that the everyday standards by which we judge bicycles or sulphur baths are applicable to philosophy.

It is absolutely correct and proper to say that "You can't do anything with philosophy." It is only wrong to suppose that this is the last word on philosophy. For the rejoinder imposes itself: granted that *we* cannot do anything with philosophy, might not philosophy, if we concern ourselves with it, do something *with us?* So much for what philosophy is not.

At the outset we stated a question: "Why are there essents rather than nothing?" We have maintained that to ask this question is to philosophize. When in our thinking we open our minds to this question, we first of all cease to dwell in any of the familiar realms. We set aside everything that is on the order of the day. Our question goes beyond the familiar and the things that have their place in everyday life. Nietzsche once said (*Werke, 7,* 269): "A philosopher is a man who never ceases to experience, see, hear, suspect, hope, and dream extraordinary things . . ."

To philosophize is to inquire into the *extra*-ordinary. But because, as we have just suggested, this questioning recoils upon itself, not only what is asked after is extraordinary but also the asking itself. In other words: this questioning does not lie along the way so that we bump into it one day unexpectedly. Nor is it part of everyday life: there is no requirement or regulation that forces us into it; it gratifies no urgent or prevailing need. The questioning itself is "out of order." It is entirely voluntary, based wholly and uniquely on the mystery of freedom, on what we have called the leap. The same Nietzsche said: "Philosophy . . . is a voluntary living amid ice and mountain heights" (*Werke, 15, 2*). To philosophize, we may now say, is an extra-ordinary inquiry into the extra-ordinary.

In the age of the earliest and crucial unfolding of Western philosophy among the Greeks, who first raised the authentic question of the essent as such in its entirety, the essent was called *physis*. This basic Greek word for the essent is customarily translated as "nature." This derives from the Latin translation, *natura*, which properly means "to be born," "birth." But with this Latin translation the original meaning of the Greek word *physis* is thrust aside, the actual philosophical force of the Greek word is destroyed. This is true not only of the Latin translation of *this* word but of all other Roman translations of the Greek philosophical language. What happened in this translation from the Greek into the Latin is not accidental and harmless; it marks the first stage in the process by which we cut ourselves off and alienated ourselves from the original essence of Greek philosophy. The Roman translation was later taken over by Christianity and the Christian Middle Ages. And the Christian Middle Ages were prolonged in modern philosophy, which, moving in the conceptual world of the Middle Ages, coined those representations and terms by means of which we still try to understand the beginnings of Western philosophy. These beginnings are regarded as something that present-day philosophers have supposedly transcended and long since left behind them.

But now let us skip over this whole process of deformation and decay and attempt to regain the unimpaired strength of language and words; for words and language are not wrappings in which things are packed for the commerce of those who write and speak. It is in words and language that things first come into being and are. For this reason the misuse of language in idle talk, in slogans and phrases, destroys our authentic relation to things. What does the word *physis* denote? It denotes self-blossoming emergence (e.g. the blossoming of a rose), opening up, unfolding, that which manifests

φύωτο blossom   φύσις

itself in such unfolding and perseveres and endures in it; in short, the realm of things that emerge and linger on. According to the dictionary *phyein* means to grow or make to grow. But what does growing mean? Does it imply only to increase quantitatively, to become more and larger?

Physis as emergence can be observed everywhere, e.g. in celestial phenomena (the rising of the sun), in the rolling of the sea, in the growth of plants, in the coming forth of man and animal from the womb. But *physis*, the realm of that which arises, is not synonymous with these phenomena, which today we regard as part of "nature." This opening up and inward-jutting-beyond-itself 〈 in-sich-aus-sich-hinausstehen 〉 must not be taken as a process among other processes that we observe in the realm of the essent. *Physis is being itself*, by virtue of which essents become and remain observable.

The Greeks did not learn what *physis* is through natural phenomena, but the other way around: it was through a fundamental poetic and intellectual experience of being that they discovered what they had to call *physis*. It was this discovery that enabled them to gain a glimpse into nature in the restricted sense. Hence *physis* originally encompassed heaven as well as earth, the stone as well as the plant, the animal as well as man, and it encompassed human history as a work of men and the gods; and ultimately and first of all, it meant the gods themselves as subordinated to destiny. *Physis* means the power that emerges and the enduring realm under its sway. This power of emerging and enduring includes "becoming" as well as "being" in the restricted sense of inert duration. *Physis* is the process of a-rising, of emerging from the hidden, whereby the hidden is first made to stand.

But if, as is usually done, *physis* is taken not in the original sense of the power to emerge and endure, but in the later and present signification of nature; and if moreover the motion of material things, of the atoms and electrons, of what modern physics investigates as *physis*, is taken to be the fundamental manifestation of nature, then the first philosophy of the Greeks becomes a nature philosophy, in which all things are held to be of a material nature. In this case the beginning of Greek philosophy, as is perfectly proper for a beginning according to the common-sense view, gives the impression of what we, once again in Latin, designate as primitive. Thus the Greeks become essentially a higher type of Hottentot, whom modern science has left far behind. Disregarding the lesser absurdities involved in this view of the beginning of Western philosophy as something primitive, we need only say this: those who put forward such an interpretation forget that what is under discussion is philosophy, one of man's few great achievements. But what is great can only begin great. Its beginning is in fact the greatest thing of all. A small beginning belongs only to the small, whose dubious greatness it is to diminish all things; small are the beginnings of decay, though it may later become great in the sense of the enormity of total annihilation.

The great begins great, maintains itself only through the free recurrence of greatness within it, and if it is great ends also in greatness. So it is with the philosophy of the Greeks. It ended in greatness with Aristotle. Only prosaic common sense and the little man imagine that the great must endure forever, and equate this duration with eternity.

The Greeks called the essent as a whole *physis*. But it should be said in passing that even within Greek philosophy a narrowing of the word set in forthwith, although the original meaning did not vanish from the experience, knowledge, and orientation of Greek philosophy. Knowledge of its original meaning still lives on in Aristotle, when he speaks of the grounds of the essent as such (see *Metaphysics*, I, 1003 a 27).

But this narrowing of *physis* in the direction of "physics" did not occur in the way that we imagine today. We oppose the psychic, the animated, the living, to the "physical." But for the Greeks all this belonged to *physis* and continued to do so even after Aristotle. They contrasted it with what they called *thesis*, thesis, ordinance, or *nomos*, law, rule in the sense of *ethos*. This, however, denotes not mere norms but mores, based on freely accepted obligations and traditions; it is that which concerns free behavior and attitudes, the shaping of man's historical being, the *ethos* which under the influence of morality was later degraded to the ethical.

The meaning of *physis* is further restricted by contrast with *technē*—which denotes neither art nor technology but a knowledge, the ability to plan and organize freely, to master institu-

tions (cf. Plato's *Phaedrus*). *Technē* is creating, building in
the sense of a deliberate pro-ducing. (It would require a special study to explain what is essentially the same in *physis* and
technē.) The physical was opposed to the historical, a domain which for the Greeks was part of the originally broader
concept of *physis*. But this has nothing whatever to do with
a naturalistic interpretation of history. The realm of being as
such and as a whole is *physis*—i.e. its essence and character
are defined as that which emerges and endures. It is experienced primarily through what in a way imposes itself most
immediately on our attention, and this was the later, narrower
sense of *physis: ta physei onta, ta physika,* nature. If the question concerning *physis* in general was asked at all, i.e. if it was
asked: What is the realm of being as such? it was primarily
ta physei onta that gave the point of departure. Yet from the
very outset the question could not dwell in this or that realm
of nature, inanimate bodies, plants, animals, but had to reach
out beyond *ta physika*.

In Greek, "beyond something" is expressed by the word
meta. Philosophical inquiry into the realm of being as such
is *meta ta physika;* this inquiry goes beyond the essent, it is
metaphysics. Here it is not important to follow the genesis
and history of this term in detail.

Accordingly, the question to which we have given first
rank, "Why are there essents rather than nothing?" is the
fundamental question of metaphysics. Metaphysics is a name
for the pivotal point and core of all philosophy.

[In this introduction our treatment of the entire subject has
been intentionally superficial and hence essentially vague.
According to our explanation of the word *physis*, it signifies
the being of the essent. If the questioning is *peri physeōs,* if
it concerns the being of the essent, then the discussion has gone
beyond *physis*, beyond "physics" in the ancient sense, and
essentially beyond *ta physika*, beyond essents, and deals with
being. From the very first "physics" has determined the essence and history of metaphysics. Even in the doctrines of
being as pure act (Thomas Aquinas), as absolute concept
(Hegel), as eternal recurrence of the identical will to power
(Nietzsche), metaphysics has remained unalterably "physics."

But the inquiry into being as such is of a different nature and origin.

Within the purview of metaphysics and thinking on its level, we can, to be sure, consider the question about being as such as merely a mechanical repetition of the question about the essent as such. In this case the question about being as such is just another transcendental question, though one of a higher order. But this reinterpretation of the question about being as such bars the road to its appropriate unfolding.

However, this new interpretation comes readily to mind; it is bound to suggest itself, particularly as we have spoken in *Sein und Zeit* of a "transcendental horizon." But the "transcendental" there intended is not that of the subjective consciousness; rather, it defines itself in terms of the existential-ecstatic temporality of human being-there. Yet the reinterpretation of the question of being as such tends to take the same form as the question of the essent as such, chiefly because the essential origin of the question of the existent as such and with it the essence of metaphysics remain obscure. And this draws all questions that are in any way concerned with being into the indeterminate.

In the present attempt at an "introduction to metaphysics" I shall keep this confused state of affairs in mind.

In the current interpretation the "question of being" signifies the inquiry into the essent as such (metaphysics). But from the standpoint of *Sein und Zeit*, the "question of being" means the inquiry into being as such. This signification of the title is also the appropriate one from the standpoint of the subject matter and of linguistics; for the "question of being" in the sense of the metaphysical question regarding the essent as such does *not inquire* thematically into being. In this way of asking, being remains forgotten.

But just as ambiguous as the "question of being" referred to in the title is what is said about "forgetfulness of being." It is pointed out—quite correctly—that metaphysics inquires into the being of the essent and that it is therefore an obvious absurdity to impute a forgetfulness of being to metaphysics.

But if we consider the question of being in the sense of an inquiry into being as such, it becomes clear to anyone who follows our thinking that being *as such* is precisely hidden from metaphysics, and remains forgotten—and so radically that the forgetfulness of being, which itself falls into forgetfulness, is the unknown but enduring impetus to metaphysical questioning.

If for the treatment of the "question of being" in the indeterminate sense we choose the name "metaphysics," then the title of the present work is ambiguous. For at first sight the questioning seems to remain within the sphere of the essent as such, yet at the very first sentence it strives to depart from this sphere in order to consider and inquire into another realm. Actually the title of the work is deliberately ambiguous.

The fundamental question of this work is of a different kind from the leading question of metaphysics. Taking what was said in *Sein und Zeit* (pp. 21 f. and 37 f.) as a starting point, we inquired into the *"disclosure of being."* "Disclosure of being" means the unlocking of what forgetfulness of being closes and hides. And it is through this questioning that a light first falls on the *essence* of metaphysics that had hitherto also been hidden.]

"Introduction to metaphysics" means accordingly: an introduction to the asking of the fundamental question. But questions and particularly fundamental questions do not just occur like stones and water. Questions are not found ready-made like shoes and clothes and books. Questions *are*, and are only as they are actually asked. A leading into the asking of the fundamental questions is consequently not a going to something that lies and stands somewhere; no, this leading-to must first awaken and create the questioning. The leading is itself a questioning advance, a preliminary questioning. It is a leading for which in the very nature of things there can be no following. When we hear of disciples, "followers," as in a school of philosophy for example, it means that the nature of questioning is misunderstood. Such schools can exist only in the domain of scientific and technical work. Here everything has its definite hierarchical order. This work is also an indispensable part of philosophy and has today been lost. But the best technical ability can never replace the actual power of seeing and inquiring and speaking.

"Why are there essents rather than nothing?" That is the

question. To state the interrogative sentence, even in a tone of questioning, is not yet to question. To repeat the interrogative sentence several times in succession does not necessarily breathe life into the questioning; on the contrary, saying the sentence over and over may well dull the questioning.

But even though the interrogative sentence is not the question and not the questioning, it must not be taken as a mere linguistic form of communication, as though, for example, the interrogative sentence were only a statement "about" a question. When I say to you "Why are there essents rather than nothing?" the purpose of my speaking and questioning is not to communicate to you the fact that a process of questioning is now at work within me. The spoken interrogative sentence can of course be interpreted in this way, but this means precisely that the questioning has not been heard. In this case you do not join me in questioning, nor do you question yourself. No sign of a questioning attitude or state of mind is awakened. Such a state of mind consists in a *willing* to know. Willing—that is no mere wishing or striving. Those who wish to know also seem to question; but they do not go beyond the stating of the question; they stop precisely where the question begins. To question is to will to know. He who wills, he who puts his whole existence into a will, *is* resolved. Resolve does not shift about; it does not shirk, but acts from out of the moment and never stops. Re-solve is no mere decision to act, but the crucial beginning of action that anticipates and reaches through all action. To will is to be resolved. [The essence of willing is here carried back to determination ⟨ Ent-schlossenheit, unclosedness ⟩. But the essence of resolve lies in the opening, the coming-out-of-cover ⟨ Ent-borgenheit ⟩ of human being-there into the clearing of being, and not in a storing up of energy for "action." See *Sein und Zeit*, § 44 and § 60. But its relation to being is one of letting-be. The idea that all willing should be grounded in letting-be offends the understanding. See my lecture *Vom Wesen der Wahrheit*, 1930.]

But to know means: to be able to stand in the truth. Truth is the manifestness of the essent. To know is accordingly the ability to stand ⟨ stehen ⟩ in the manifestness of the essent, to endure ⟨ bestehen ⟩ it. Merely to have information, however abundant, is not to know. Even if curricula and examination requirements concentrate this information into what is of the greatest practical importance, it still does not amount to knowledge. Even if this information, pruned down to the most indispensable needs, is "close to life," its possession is not knowledge. The man who possesses such information and has learned a few practical tricks, will still be perplexed in the presence of real reality, which is always different from what the philistine means by down-to-earth; he will always be a bungler. Why? Because he has no knowledge, for to know means *to be able to learn.*

In the common-sense view, to be sure, knowledge belongs to the man who has no further need to learn because he has finished learning. No, only that man is knowing who understands that he must keep learning over and over again and who above all, on the basis of this understanding, has attained to the point where he is always *able to learn.* This is much more difficult than to possess information.

Ability to learn presupposes ability to inquire. Inquiry is the willing-to-know analyzed above: the resolve to be able to stand in the openness of the essent. Since we are concerned with the asking of the question that is first in rank, clearly the willing as well as the knowing is of a very special kind. So much the less will the interrogative sentence, even if it is uttered in an authentically questioning tone and even if the listener joins in the questioning, exhaustively reproduce the question. The questioning, which indeed is sounded in the interrogative sentence but which is still enclosed, wrapped up in the words, remains to be unwrapped. The questioning attitude must clarify and secure itself in this process, it must be consolidated by training.

Our next task lies in the development of the question "Why are there essents rather than nothing?" In what direction can it be asked? First of all the question is accessible in the interrogative sentence, which gives a kind of approximation of it. Hence its linguistic formulation must be correspondingly broad and loose. Let us consider our sentence in this respect. "Why are there essents rather than nothing?" The sentence has a caesura. "Why are there essents?" With these words the question is actually asked. The formulation of the question includes: 1) a definite indication of what is put into question, of what is *questioned;* 2) an indication of what the question is about, of what is asked. For it is clearly indicated what the question is about, namely the essent. What is asked after, that which is asked, is the why, i.e. the ground. What follows in the interrogative sentence, "rather than nothing," is only an appendage, which may be said to turn up of its own accord if for purposes of introduction we permit ourselves to speak loosely, a turn of phrase that says nothing further about the question or the object of questioning, an ornamental flourish. Actually the question is far more unambiguous and definite without such an appendage, which springs only from the prolixity of loose discourse. "Why are there essents?" The addition "rather than nothing" is dropped not only because we are striving for a strict formulation of the question but even more because it says nothing. For why should we go on to ask about nothing? Nothing is simply nothing. Here there is nothing more to inquire about. And above all, in talking about nothing or nothingness, we are not making the slightest advance toward the knowledge of the essent.

He who speaks of nothing does not know what he is doing. In speaking of nothing he makes it into a something. In speaking he speaks against what he intended. He contradicts himself. But discourse that contradicts itself offends against the fundamental rule of discourse (*logos*), against "logic." To speak of nothing is illogical. He who speaks and thinks illogically is unscientific. But he who goes so far as to speak of nothing in the realm of philosophy, where logic has its very home, exposes himself most particularly to the accusation of offending against the fundamental rule of all thinking. Such a speaking about nothing consists entirely of meaningless propositions. Moreover: he who takes the nothing seriously is allying himself with nothingness. He is patently promoting the spirit of negation and serving the cause of disintegration. Not only is speaking of nothing utterly repellent to thought; it also undermines all culture and all faith. What disregards the fundamental law of thought and also destroys faith and the will to build is pure nihilism.

On the basis of such considerations we shall do well, in our interrogative sentence, to cross out the superfluous words *re formulation of the question*

"rather than nothing" and limit the sentence to the simple and
strict form: "Why are there essents?"

To this there would be no objection if . . . if in formulat-
ing our question, if altogether, in the asking of this question,
we were as free as it may have seemed to us up to this point.
But in asking this question we stand in a tradition. For philosophy has always, from time immemorial, asked about the
ground of what is. With this question it began and with this
question it will end, provided that it ends in greatness and
not in an impotent decline. Ever since the question about the
essent began, the question about the nonessent, about nothing,
has gone side by side with it. And not only outwardly, in the
manner of a by-product. Rather, the question about nothing
has been asked with the same breadth, depth, and originality
as the question about the essent. The manner of asking about
nothing may be regarded as a gauge and hallmark for the
manner of asking about the essent.

If we bear this in mind, the interrogative sentence uttered
in the beginning, "Why are there essents rather than nothing?"
seems to express the question about the essent far more adequately than the abbreviated version. It is not looseness of
speech or prolixity that leads us to mention nothing. Nor is it
an invention of ours; no, it is only strict observance of the
original tradition regarding the meaning of the fundamental
question.

Still, this speaking of nothing remains in general repellent
to thought and in particular demoralizing. But what if both
our concern for the fundamental rules of thought and our
fear of nihilism, which both seem to counsel against speaking
of nothing, should be based on a misunderstanding? And this
indeed is the case. True, this misunderstanding is not accidental. It is rooted in long years of failure to understand the
question about the essent. And this failure to understand arises
from an increasingly hardened forgetfulness of being.

For it cannot be decided out of hand whether logic and its
fundamental rules can, altogether, provide a standard for dealing with the question about the essent as such. It might be
the other way around. Perhaps the whole body of logic as it
is known to us, perhaps all the logic that we treat as a gift
from heaven, is grounded in a very definite answer to the

Thinking about nothing

question about the essent; perhaps, in consequence, all thinking which solely follows the laws of thought prescribed by
traditional logic is incapable from the very start of even understanding the question about the essent by its own resources, let alone actually unfolding the question and guiding
it toward an answer. Actually it is only an appearance of
strict, scientific method when we invoke the principle of contradiction and logic in general, in order to prove that all
thinking and speaking about nothing are contradictory and
therefore meaningless. In such a contention "logic" is regarded as a court of justice, established for all eternity, whose
rights as first and last authority no rational man will impugn.
Anyone who speaks against logic is therefore tacitly or explicitly accused of irresponsibility. And the mere accusation
is taken as a proof and an argument relieving one of the need
for any further, genuine reflection.   *scientific thought*

It is perfectly true that we cannot talk about nothing, as
though it were a thing like the rain outside or a mountain or
any object whatsoever. In principle, nothingness remains inaccessible to science. The man who wishes truly to speak
about nothing must of necessity become unscientific. But this
is a misfortune only so long as one supposes that scientific
thinking is the only authentic rigorous thought, and that it
alone can and must be made into the standard of philosophical thinking. But the reverse is true. All scientific thought is
merely a derived form of philosophical thinking, which proceeded to freeze into its scientific cast. Philosophy never arises
out of science or through science and it can never be accorded
equal rank with the sciences. No, it is prior in rank, and not
only "logically" or in a table representing the system of the
sciences. Philosophy stands in a totally different realm and
order. Only poetry stands in the same order as philosophy   *poetry*
and its thinking, though poetry and thought are not the same
thing. To speak of nothing will always remain a horror and
an absurdity for science. But aside from the philosopher, the
poet can do so—and not because, as common sense supposes,
poetry is without strict rules, but because the spirit of poetry
(only authentic and great poetry is meant) is essentially superior to the spirit that prevails in all mere science. By virtue
of this superiority the poet always speaks as though the essent

were being expressed and invoked for the first time. Poetry, like the thinking of the philosopher, has always so much world space to spare that in it each thing—a tree, a mountain, a house, the cry of a bird—loses all indifference and commonplaceness.

Authentic speaking about nothing always remains extraordinary. It cannot be vulgarized. It dissolves if it is placed in the cheap acid of a merely logical intelligence. Consequently true discourse about nothing can never be immediate like the description of a picture for example. Here I should like to cite a passage from one of Knut Hamsun's last works, *The Road Leads On.* The work forms a whole with *Vagabonds* and *August.* It describes the last years and end of this August, who embodies the uprooted modern man who can do everything equally well yet who cannot lose his ties with the extraordinary, because even in his weakness and despair he remains authentic and superior. In his last days August is alone in the high mountains. And the poet says: "Here he sits between his ears and all he hears is emptiness. An amusing conception, indeed. On the sea there were both motion and sound, something for the ear to feed upon, a chorus of waters. Here nothingness meets nothingness and the result is zero, not even a hole. Enough to make one shake one's head, utterly at a loss."*

We see that there is something very interesting about nothing. Let us then go back to our interrogative sentence; let us ask it through, and see whether this "rather than nothing" is merely a meaningless appendage or whether it does not have an essential meaning even in our provisional statement of the question.

Let us begin with the abbreviated, seemingly simpler, and ostensibly stricter form of the question: "Why are there essents?" When we inquire in this way, we start from the essent. The essent *is.* It is given, it confronts us; accordingly, it is to be found at any time, and it is, in certain realms, known to us. Now this essent, from which we start, is immediately questioned as to its ground. The questioning advances immediately toward a ground. Such a method is only an ex-

---

* Knut Hamsun, *The Road Leads On* (Coward-McCann, 1934), p. 508. Trans. Eugene Gay-Tifft.

tension and enlargement, so to speak, of a method practiced in everyday life. Somewhere in the vineyard, for example, the vine-disease occurs; something incontestably present. We ask: where does it come from, where and what is the reason for it, the ground? Similarly the essent as a whole is present. We ask: where and what is the ground? This manner of questioning is represented in the simple formula: Why are there essents? Where and what is their ground? Tacitly we are asking after another and higher kind of essent. But here the question is not by any means concerned with the essent as such and as a whole.

But if we put the question in the form of our original interrogative sentence: "Why are there essents rather than nothing?" this addition prevents us in our questioning from beginning directly with an unquestionably given essent and, having scarcely begun, from continuing on to another expected essent as a ground. Instead this essent, through questioning, is held out into the possibility of nonbeing. Thereby the why takes on a very different power and penetration. Why is the essent torn away from the possibility of nonbeing? Why does it not simply keep falling back into nonbeing? Now the essent is no longer that which just happens to be present; it begins to waver and oscillate, regardless of whether or not we recognize the essent in all certainty, regardless of whether or not we apprehend it in its full scope. Henceforth the essent as such oscillates, insofar as we draw it into the question. The swing of the pendulum extends to the extreme and sharpest contrary possibility, to nonbeing and nothingness. And the search for the why undergoes a parallel change. It does not aim simply at providing an also present ground and explanation for what is present; now a ground is sought which will explain the emergence of the essent as an overcoming of nothingness. The ground that is now asked after is the ground of the decision for the essent over against nothingness, or more precisely, the ground for the oscillation of the essent, which sustains and unbinds us, half being, half not being, which is also why we can belong entirely to nothing, not even to ourselves; yet being-there ⟨ Dasein ⟩ is in every case mine.

overcoming nothingness

[The qualification "in every case mine" means that being-there is allotted to me in order that my self should be being-there. But being-there signifies: care of the ecstatically manifested being of the essent as such, not only of human being. Being-there is "in every case mine"; this means neither "posited through me" nor "apportioned to an individual ego." Being-there is *itself* by virtue of its essential relation to being in general. That is the meaning of the sentence that occurs frequently in *Sein und Zeit*: Being-there implies awareness of being.]

It is already becoming clearer that this "rather than nothing" is no superfluous appendage to the real question, but is an essential component of the whole interrogative sentence, which as a whole states an entirely different question from that intended in the question "Why are there essents?" With our question we place ourselves in the essent in such a way that it loses its self-evident character *as the essent*. The essent begins to waver between the broadest and most drastic extremes: "either essents—or nothing"—and thereby the questioning itself loses all solid foundation. Our questioning being-there is suspended, and in this suspense is nevertheless self-sustained.

But the essent is not changed by our questioning. It remains what it is and as it is. Our questioning is after all only a psycho-spiritual process in us which, whatever course it may take, cannot in any way affect the essent itself. True, the essent remains as it is manifested to us. But it cannot slough off the problematic fact that it might also *not* be what it is and as it is. We do not experience this possibility as something that we add to the essent by thinking; rather, the essent itself elicits this possibility, and in this possibility reveals itself. Our questioning only opens up the horizon, in order that the essent may dawn in such questionableness.

We still know far too little about the process of such questioning, and what we do know is far too crude. In this questioning we seem to belong entirely to ourselves. Yet it is this questioning that moves us into the open, provided that in questioning it transform itself (which all true questioning does), and cast a new space over everything and into everything.

The main thing is not to let ourselves be led astray by over-hasty theories, but to experience things as they are on the basis of the first thing that comes to hand. This piece of chalk has extension; it is a relatively solid, grayish white thing with a definite shape, and apart from all that, it is a thing to write with. This particular thing has the attribute of lying here; but just as surely, it has the attribute of potentially not lying here and not being so large. The possibility of being guided along the blackboard and of being used up is not something that we add to the thing by thought. Itself, as this essent, is in this possibility; otherwise it would not be chalk as a writing material. Correspondingly, every essent has in it this potentiality in a different way. This potentiality belongs to the chalk. It has in itself a definite aptitude for a definite use. True, we are accustomed and inclined, in seeking this potentiality in the chalk, to say that we cannot see or touch it. But that is a prejudice, the elimination of which is part of the unfolding of our question. For the present our question is only to open up the essent in its wavering between nonbeing and being. Insofar as the essent resists the extreme possibility of nonbeing, it stands in being, but it has never caught up with or overcome the possibility of nonbeing.

We suddenly find ourselves speaking of the nonbeing and being of the essent, without saying how this being or nonbeing is related to the essent. Are the two terms the same? The essent and its being? What, for example, is "the essent" in this piece of chalk? The very question is ambiguous, because the word "the essent" can be understood in two respects, like the Greek *to on*. The essent means first *that* which is at any time, in particular this grayish white, so-and-so-shaped, light, brittle mass. But "the essent" also means that which "brings it about," so to speak, that this thing is an essent rather than a nonessent, that which constitutes its being if it *is*. In accordance with this twofold meaning of the word "the essent," the Greek *to on* often has the second significance, not the essent itself, not that which is, but "is-ness," essentness, being. Over against this, "the essent" in the first sense signifies all or particular essent things themselves, in respect to themselves and not to their is-ness, their *ousia*.

The first meaning of *to on* refers to *ta onta* (entia), the second to *to einai* (esse). We have listed what the essent is

contingency of τὰ ὄντα, essents

in the piece of chalk. This was relatively easy to do. It was also easy to see that the object named can also *not* be, that this chalk need ultimately not be here and not be. What then is being in distinction to what can stand in being or fall back into nonbeing—what is being in distinction to the essent? Is it the same as the essent? We ask the question once again. But in the foregoing we did not list being; we listed only material mass, grayish-white light, so-and-so-shaped, brittle. But where is the being situated? It must belong to the chalk, for this chalk *is*.

We encounter the essent everywhere; it sustains and drives us, enchants and fills us, elevates and disappoints us; but with all this, where is, and wherein consists, the being of the essent? One might reply: this distinction between the essent and its being may occasionally have an importance from the standpoint of language and even of meaning; this distinction can be effected in mere thought, i.e. in ideas and opinions, but is it certain that anything essent in the essent corresponds to the distinction? And even this merely cogitated distinction is questionable; for it remains unclear *what* is to be thought under the name of "being." Meanwhile it suffices to know the essent and secure our mastery over it. To go further and introduce being as distinct from it is artificial and leads to nothing.

We have already said a certain amount about this frequent question: What comes of such distinctions? Here we are going to concentrate on our undertaking. We ask: "Why are there essents rather than nothing?" And in this question we seemingly stick to the essent and avoid all empty brooding about being. But what really are we asking? Why the essent as such is. We are asking for the ground of the essent: that it is and is what it is, and that there is not rather nothing. Fundamentally we are asking about being. But how? We are asking about the being of the essent. We are questioning the essent in regard to its being.

But if we persevere in our questioning we shall actually be questioning forward, asking about being in respect to its ground, even if this question remains undeveloped and it remains undecided whether being itself is not in itself a ground and a sufficient ground. If we regard this question of being as the first question in order of rank, should we ask it without knowing how it stands with being and how being stands in its distinction to the essent? How shall we inquire into, not to say find, the ground for the being of the essent, if we have not adequately considered and understood being itself? This undertaking would be just as hopeless as if someone were to try to bring out the cause and ground of a fire, and yet claim that he need not worry about the actual course of the fire or examine the scene of it.

Thus it transpires that the question "Why are there essents rather than nothing?" compels us to ask the preliminary question: "How does it stand with being?"

Here we are asking about something which we barely grasp, which is scarcely more than the sound of a word for us, and which puts us in danger of serving a mere word idol when we proceed with our questioning. Hence it is all the more indispensable that we make it clear from the very outset how it stands at present with being and with our understanding of being. And in this connection the main thing is to impress it on our experience that we cannot immediately grasp the being of the essent itself, either through the essent or in the essent—or anywhere else.

Example

A few examples may be helpful. Over there, across the street, stands the high school building. An essent. We can look over the building from all sides, we can go in and explore it from cellar to attic, and note everything we encounter in that building: corridors, staircases, schoolrooms, and their equipment. Everywhere we find essents and we even find them in a very definite arrangement. Now where is the being of this high school? For after all it *is*. The building *is*. If anything belongs to this essent, it is its being; yet we do not find the being inside it.

perception

Nor does the being consist in the fact that we look at the essent. The building stands there even if we do not look at it. We can find it only because it already *is*. Moreover, this building's being does not by any means seem to be the same for everyone. For us, who look at it or ride by, it is different than for the pupils who sit in it; not because they see it only from within but because for them this building really is what it is and as it is. You can, as it were, smell the being of this

Wherein consists the being?

building in your nostrils. The smell communicates the being
of this essent far more immediately and truly than any description or inspection could ever do. But on the other hand
the building's being is not based on this odor that is somewhere in the air.

How does it stand with being? Can you see being? We see
essents; this chalk for example. But do we see being as we
see color and light and shade? Or do we hear, smell, taste,
feel being? We hear the motorcycle racing through the street.
We hear the grouse gliding through the forest. But actually
we hear only the whirring of the motor, the sound the grouse
makes. As a matter of fact it is difficult to describe even the
pure sound, and we do not ordinarily do so, because it is *not*
what we commonly hear. [From the standpoint of sheer
sound] we always hear *more*. We hear the flying bird, even
though strictly speaking we should say: a grouse is nothing
audible, it is no manner of tone that fits into a scale. And
so it is with the other senses. We touch velvet, silk; we see
them directly as this and that kind of essent, the one different
from the other. Wherein lies and wherein consists being?

But we must take a wider look around us and consider the
lesser and greater circle within which we spend our days
and hours, wittingly and wittingly, a circle whose limits shift
continuously and which is suddenly broken through.

A heavy storm coming up in the mountains "is," or what
here amounts to the same thing, "was" during the night.
Wherein consists its being?

A distant mountain range under a broad sky . . . It "is."
Wherein consists the being? When and to whom does it reveal itself? To the traveler who enjoys the landscape, or to
the peasant who makes his living in it and from it, or to the
meteorologist who is preparing a weather report? Who of
these apprehends being? All and none. Or is what these men
apprehend of the mountain range under the great sky only
certain aspects of it, not the mountain range itself as it "is"
as such, not that wherein its actual being consists? Who may
be expected to apprehend this being? Or is it a non-sense,
contrary to the sense of being, to inquire after what is in
itself, behind those aspects? Does the being lie in the aspects?

The door of an early romanesque church is an essent. How

and to whom is its being revealed? To the connoisseur of art, who examines it and photographs it on an excursion, or to the abbot who on a holiday passes through this door with his monks, or to the children who play in its shadow on a summer's day? How does it stand with the being of this essent?

A state—*is*. By virtue of the fact that the state police arrest a suspect, or that so-and-so-many typewriters are clattering in a government building, taking down the words of ministers and state secretaries? Or "is" the state in a conversation between the chancellor and the British foreign minister? The state *is*. But where is being situated? Is it situated anywhere at all? *the elusiveness of being*

A painting by Van Gogh. A pair of rough peasant shoes, nothing else. Actually the painting represents nothing. But as to what *is* in that picture, you are immediately alone with it as though you yourself were making your way wearily homeward with your hoe on an evening in late fall after the last potato fires have died down. What *is* here? The canvas? The brush strokes? The spots of color?

What in all these things we have just mentioned is the being of the essent? We run (or stand) around in the world with our silly subtleties and conceit. But where in all this is being?

All the things we have named *are* and yet—when we wish to apprehend being, it is always as though we were reaching into the void. The being after which we inquire is almost like nothing, and yet we have always rejected the contention that the essent in its entirety *is not*.

But being remains unfindable, almost like nothing, or ultimately *quite* so. Then, in the end, the word "being" is no more than an empty word. It means nothing real, tangible, material. Its meaning is an unreal vapor. Thus in the last analysis Nietzsche was perfectly right in calling such "highest concepts" as being "the last cloudy streak of evaporating reality." Who would want to chase after such a vapor, when the very term is merely a name for a great fallacy! "Nothing indeed has exercised a more simple power of persuasion hitherto than the error of Being . . ."*

* *The Twilight of Idols*, Nietzsche's Complete Works, Edinburgh and London, *16* (1911), 19, 22.

nietzsche!

"Being"—a vapor and a fallacy? What Nietzsche says here of being is no random remark thrown out in the frenzy of preparation for his central, never finished work. No, this was his guiding view of being from the earliest days of his philosophical effort. It is the fundamental support and determinant of his philosophy. Yet even now this philosophy holds its ground against all the crude importunities of the scribblers who cluster round him more numerous with each passing day. And so far there seems to be no end in sight to this abuse of Nietzsche's work. In speaking here of Nietzsche, we mean to have nothing to do with all that—or with blind hero worship for that matter. The task in hand is too crucial and at the same time too sobering. It consists first of all, if we are to gain a true grasp of Nietzsche, in bringing his accomplishment to a full unfolding. Being a vapor, a fallacy? If this were so, the only possible consequence would be to abandon the question "Why are there essents as such and as a whole, rather than nothing?" For what good is the question if what it inquires into is only a vapor and a fallacy?

Does Nietzsche speak the truth? Or was he himself only the last victim of a long process of error and neglect, but as such the unrecognized witness to a new necessity?

Is it the fault of being that it is so involved? is it the fault of the word that it remains so empty? or are we to blame that with all our effort, with all our chasing after the essent, we have fallen out of being? And should we not say that the fault did not begin with us, or with our immediate or more remote ancestors, but lies in something that runs through Western history from the very beginning, a happening which the eyes of all the historians in the world will never perceive, but which nevertheless happens, which happened in the past and will happen in the future? What if it were possible that man, that nations in their greatest movements and traditions, are linked to being and yet had long fallen out of being, without knowing it, and that this was the most powerful and most central cause of their decline? (See *Sein und Zeit*, § 38, in particular pp. 179 f.)

We do not ask these questions incidentally, and still less do they spring from any particular outlook or state of mind; no, they are questions to which we are driven by that pre-

Is being in a vapor or ... the spiritual destiny ...?

liminary question which sprang necessarily from our main question "How does it stand with being?"—a sober question perhaps, but assuredly a very useless one. And yet a *question, the* question: is "being" a mere word and its meaning a vapor or is it the spiritual destiny of the Western world?

This Europe, in its ruinous blindness forever on the point of cutting its own throat, lies today in a great pincers, squeezed between Russia on one side and America on the other. From a metaphysical point of view, Russia and America are the same; the same dreary technological frenzy, the same unrestricted organization of the average man. At a time when the farthermost corner of the globe has been conquered by technology and opened to economic exploitation; when any incident whatever, regardless of where or when it occurs, can be communicated to the rest of the world at any desired speed; when the assassination of a king in France and a symphony concert in Tokyo can be "experienced" simultaneously; when time has ceased to be anything other than velocity, instantaneousness, and simultaneity, and time as history has vanished from the lives of all peoples; when a boxer is regarded as a nation's great man; when mass meetings attended by millions are looked on as a triumph—then, yes then, through all this turmoil a question still haunts us like a specter: What for?— Whither?—And what then? *spiritual decline*

The spiritual decline of the earth is so far advanced that the nations are in danger of losing the last bit of spiritual energy that makes it possible to see the decline (taken in relation to the history of "being"), and to appraise it as such. This simple observation has nothing to do with *Kulturpessimismus,* and of course it has nothing to do with any sort of optimism either; for the darkening of the world, the flight of the gods, the destruction of the earth, the transformation of men into a mass, the hatred and suspicion of everything free and creative, have assumed such proportions throughout the earth that such childish categories as pessimism and optimism have long since become absurd.

We are caught in a pincers. Situated in the center, our nation incurs the severest pressure. It is the nation with the most neighbors and hence the most endangered. With all this, it is the most metaphysical of nations. We are certain of this vo-

German paranoia, which fed Nazism!

cation, but our people will only be able to wrest a destiny from it if *within itself* it creates a resonance, a possibility of resonance for this vocation, and takes a creative view of its tradition. All this implies that this nation, as a historical nation, must move itself and thereby the history of the West beyond the center of their future "happening" and into the primordial realm of the powers of being. If the great decision regarding Europe is not to bring annihilation, that decision must be made in terms of new spiritual energies unfolding historically from out of the center.

To ask "How does it stand with being?" means nothing less than to recapture, to repeat ⟨ wieder-holen ⟩, the beginning of our historical-spiritual existence, in order to transform it into a new beginning. This is possible. It is indeed the crucial form of history, because it begins in the fundamental event. But we do not repeat a beginning by reducing it to something past and now known, which need merely be imitated; no, the beginning must be begun again, more radically, with all the strangeness, darkness, insecurity that attend a true beginning. Repetition as we understand it is anything but an improved continuation with the old methods of what has been up to now.

The question "How is it with being?" is included as a preliminary question in our central question "Why are there essents rather than nothing?" If we now begin to look into that which is questioned in our preliminary question, namely being, the full truth of Nietzsche's dictum is at once apparent. For if we look closely, what more is "being" to us than a mere word, an indeterminate meaning, intangible as a vapor? Nietzsche's judgment, to be sure, was meant in a purely disparaging sense. For him "being" is a delusion that should never have come about. Is "being," then, indeterminate, vague as a vapor? It is indeed. But we do not mean to sidestep this fact. On the contrary, we must see how much of a fact it is if we are to perceive its full implication.

Our questioning brings us into the landscape we must inhabit as a basic prerequisite, if we are to win back our roots in history. We shall have to ask why this fact, that for us "being" is no more than a word and a vapor, should have arisen precisely today, or whether and why it has existed for a long time. We must learn to see that this fact is not as harmless as it seems at first sight. For ultimately what matters is not that the word "being" remains a mere sound and its meaning a vapor, but that we have fallen away from what this word says and for the moment cannot find our way back; that it is for this and no other reason that the word "being" no longer applies to anything, that everything, if we merely take hold of it, dissolves like a tatter of cloud in the sunlight. Because this is so—that is why we ask about being. And we *ask* because we know that truths have never fallen into any nation's lap. The fact that people still cannot and do not wish to understand this question, even if it is asked in a still more fundamental form, deprives the question of none of its cogency.

Of course we can, seemingly with great astuteness and perspicacity, revive the old familiar argument to the effect that "being" is the most universal of concepts, that it covers anything and everything, even the nothing which also, in the sense that it is thought or spoken, "is" something. Beyond the domain of this most universal concept "being," there is, in the strictest sense of the word, nothing more, on the basis of which being itself could be more closely determined. The concept of being is an ultimate. Moreover, there is a law of logic that says: the more comprehensive a concept is—and what could be more comprehensive than the concept of "being"?—the more indeterminate and empty is its content.

For every normally thinking man—and we all should like to be normal men—this reasoning is immediately and wholly convincing. But the question now arises: does the designation of being as the most universal concept strike the essence of being, or is it not from the very outset such a misinterpretation that all questioning becomes hopeless? This then is the question: can being be regarded only as the most universal concept which inevitably occurs in all special concepts, or is being of an entirely different essence, and hence anything but an object of "ontology," provided we take this word in its traditional sense?

The word "ontology" was first coined in the seventeenth century. It marks the development of the traditional doctrine of the essent into a discipline of philosophy and a branch of

ontology

the philosophical system. But the traditional doctrine was an academic classification and ordering of what for Plato and Aristotle and again for Kant was a question, though no longer to be sure a primordial one. And it is in this sense that the word "ontology" is used today. Under this title each school of philosophy has set up and described a branch within its system. But we can also take the word "ontology" in the "broadest sense," "without reference to ontological directions and tendencies" (cf. *Sein und Zeit*, p. 11 top). In this case "ontology" signifies the endeavor to make being manifest itself, and to do so by way of the question "how does it stand with being?" (and not only with the essent as such). But since thus far this question has not even been heard, let alone echoed; since it has been expressly rejected by the various schools of academic philosophy, which strive for an "ontology" in the traditional sense, it may be preferable to dispense in the future with the terms "ontology" and "ontological." Two modes of questioning which, as we now see clearly, are worlds apart, should not bear the same name.

We ask the questions "How does it stand with being?" "What is the meaning of being?" *not* in order to set up an ontology on the traditional style, much less to criticize the past mistakes of ontology. We are concerned with something totally different: to restore man's historical being-there—and that always includes our own future being-there in the totality of the history allotted to us—to the domain of being, which it was originally incumbent on man to open up for himself. All this, to be sure, in the limits within which philosophy can accomplish anything.

Out of the fundamental question of metaphysics, "Why are there essents rather than nothing?" we have separated the preliminary question, "How does it stand with being?" The relation between the two questions requires clarification, for it is of a special kind. Ordinarily a preliminary question is dealt with before and outside the main question, though in reference to it. But, in principle, philosophical questions are never dealt with as though we might some day cast them aside. Here the preliminary question is not by any means outside of the main question; rather, it is the flame which burns as it were in the asking of the fundamental question; it is the

testing /
Europe

flaming center of all questioning. That is to say: it is crucial for the first asking of the fundamental question that in asking its *preliminary* question we derive the decisive fundamental attitude that is here essential. That is why we have related the question of being to the destiny of Europe, where the destiny of the earth is being decided—while our own historic being-there proves to be the center for Europe itself.

The question is:

Is being a mere word and its meaning a vapor, or does what is designated by the word "being" hold within it the historical destiny of the West?

To many ears the question may sound violent and exaggerated: for one might in a pinch suppose that a discussion of the question of being might be related in some very remote and indirect way to the decisive historical question of the earth, but assuredly not that the basic position and attitude of our questioning might be directly determined by the history of the human spirit on earth. And yet this relationship exists. Since our purpose is to set in motion the asking of the preliminary question, we must now show that, and to what extent, the asking of this question is an immediate and fundamental factor in the crucial historical question. For this demonstration it is necessary to anticipate an essential insight in the form of an assertion. HISTORICAL QUEST.

We maintain that this preliminary question and with it the fundamental question of metaphysics are historical questions through and through. But do not metaphysics and philosophy thereby become a historical science? Historical science after all investigates the temporal, while philosophy investigates the timeless. Philosophy is historical only insofar as it—like every work of the spirit—realizes itself in time. But in this sense the designation of metaphysical questioning as historical cannot characterize metaphysics, but merely expresses something obvious. Accordingly, the assertion is either meaningless and superfluous or else impossible, because it creates an amalgam of two fundamentally different kinds of science: philosophy and historical science.

In answer to this it must be said:

1. Metaphysics and philosophy are not sciences at all, and

the fact that their questioning is basically historical cannot make them so.

2. Historical science does not determine a fundamental relation to history, but always presupposes such a relation. It is only for this reason that historical science can distort men's relation to history, which itself is always historical; or misinterpret it and degrade it to a mere knowledge of antiquities; or else deal with crucial fields in the light of this once established relation to history, and so produce cogent history. A historical relation between our historical being-there and history may become an object of knowledge and mark an advanced state of knowledge; but it need not. Moreover, all relations to history cannot be scientifically objectified and given a place in science, and it is precisely the essential ones that cannot. Historical science can never produce the historical relation to history. It can only illuminate a relation once supplied, ground it in knowledge, which is indeed an absolute necessity for the historical being-there of a wise people, and not either an "advantage" or a "disadvantage." Because it is only in philosophy—*as distinguished from all science*—that essential relations to the realm of what is take shape, this relation *can*, indeed *must*, for us today be a fundamentally historical one.

But for an understanding of our assertion that the "metaphysical" asking of the preliminary question is historical through and through, it is above all necessary to consider this: for us history is not synonymous with the past; for the past is precisely what is no longer happening. And much less is history the merely contemporary, which never happens but merely "passes," comes and goes by. History as happening is an acting and being acted upon which pass through the *present*, which are determined from out of the future, and which take over the past. It is precisely the present that vanishes in happening.

Our asking of the fundamental question of metaphysics is historical because it opens up the process of human being-there in its essential relations—i.e. its relations to the essent as such and as a whole—opens it up to unasked possibilities, futures, and at the same time binds it back to its past beginning, so sharpening it and giving it weight in its present. In *darkening of the world.* [handwritten marginalia]

this questioning our being-there is summoned to its history in the full sense of the word, called to history and to a decision in history. And this not after the fact, in the sense that we draw ethical, ideological lessons from it. No, the basic attitude of the questioning is in itself historical; it stands and maintains itself in happening, inquiring out of happening for the sake of happening.

But we have not yet come to the essential reason why this inherently historical asking of the question about being is actually an integral part of history on earth. We have said that the world is darkening. The essential episodes of this darkening are: the flight of the gods, the destruction of the earth, the standardization of man, the pre-eminence of the mediocre.

What do we mean by world when we speak of a darkening of the world? World is always world of the *spirit*. The animal has no world nor any environment ⟨ Umwelt ⟩. Darkening of the world means emasculation of the spirit, the disintegration, wasting away, repression, and misinterpretation of the spirit. We shall attempt to explain the emasculation of the spirit in one respect, that of misinterpretation. We have said: Europe lies in a pincers between Russia and America, which are metaphysically the same, namely in regard to their world character and their relation to the spirit. What makes the situation of Europe all the more catastrophic is that this enfeeblement of the spirit originated in Europe itself and—though prepared by earlier factors—was definitively determined by its own spiritual situation in the first half of the nineteenth century. It was then that occurred what is popularly and succinctly called the "collapse of German idealism." This formula is a kind of shield behind which the already dawning spiritlessness, the dissolution of the spiritual energies, the rejection of all original inquiry into grounds and men's bond with the grounds, are hidden and masked. It was not German idealism that collapsed; rather, the age was no longer strong enough to stand up to the greatness, breadth, and originality of that spiritual world, i.e. truly to realize it, for to realize a philosophy means something very different from applying theorems and insights. The lives of men began to slide into a world which lacked that depth from out of which

the essential always comes to man and comes back to man,
so compelling him to become superior and making him act
in conformity to a rank. All things sank to the same level, a
surface resembling a blind mirror that no longer reflects, that
casts nothing back. The prevailing dimension became that
of extension and number. Intelligence no longer meant a
wealth of talent, lavishly spent, and the command of energies, but only what could be learned by everyone, the practice
of a routine, always associated with a certain amount of sweat
and a certain amount of show. In America and in Russia this
development grew into a boundless etcetera of indifference
and always-the-sameness—so much so that the quantity took
on a quality of its own. Since then the domination in those
countries of a cross section of the indifferent mass has become something more than a dreary accident. It has become
an active onslaught that destroys all rank and every world-
creating impulse of the spirit, and calls it a lie. This is the
onslaught of what we call the demonic (in the sense of destructive evil). There are many indications of the emergence
of this demonism, identical with the increasing helplessness
and uncertainty of Europe against it and within itself. One
of these signs is the emasculation of the spirit through misinterpretation; we are still in the midst of this process. This
misinterpretation of the spirit may be described briefly in
four aspects.

1. The crux of the matter is the reinterpretation of the
spirit as *intelligence,* or mere cleverness in examining and
calculating given things and the possibility of changing them
and complementing them to make new things. This cleverness
is a matter of mere talent and practice and mass division of
labor. The cleverness itself is subject to the possibility of organization, which is never true of the spirit. The attitude of the
littérateur and esthete is merely a late consequence and vari-
ation of the spirit falsified into intelligence. Mere intelligence
is a semblance of spirit, masking its absence.

2. The spirit falsified into intelligence thus falls to the level
of a tool in the service of others, a tool the manipulation of
which can be taught and learned. Whether this use of intelligence relates to the regulation and domination of the material conditions of production (as in Marxism) or in general

to the intelligent ordering and explanation of everything that is present and already posited at any time (as in positivism), or whether it is applied to the organization and regulation of a nation's vital resources and race—in any case the spirit as intelligence becomes the impotent superstructure of something else, which, because it is without spirit or even opposed to the spirit, is taken for the actual reality. If the spirit is taken as intelligence, as is done in the most extreme form of Marxism, then it is perfectly correct to say, in defense against it, that in the order of the effective forces of human being-there, the spirit, i.e. intelligence, must always be ranked below healthy physical activity and character. But this order becomes false once we understand the true essence of the spirit. For all true power and beauty of the body, all sureness and boldness in combat, all authenticity and inventiveness of the understanding, are grounded in the spirit and rise or fall only through the power or impotence of the spirit. The spirit is the sustaining, dominating principle, the first and the last, not merely an indispensable third factor.

3. As soon as the misinterpretation sets in that degrades the spirit to a tool, the energies of the spiritual process, poetry and art, statesmanship and religion, become subject to *conscious* cultivation and planning. They are split into branches. The spiritual world becomes culture and the individual strives to perfect himself in the creation and preservation of this culture. These branches become fields of free endeavor, which sets its own standards and barely manages to live up to them. These standards of production and consumption are called values. The cultural values preserve their meaning only by restricting themselves to an autonomous field: poetry for the sake of poetry, art for the sake of art, science for the sake of science.

Let us consider the example of science, which is of particular concern to us here at the university. The state of science since the turn of the century—it has remained unchanged despite a certain amount of house cleaning—is easy to see. Though today two seemingly different conceptions of science seem to combat one another—science as technical, practical, professional knowledge and science as cultural value per se— both are moving along the same downgrade of misinterpreta-

2 views of Wissenschaft

Criticism of the University

tion and emasculation of the spirit. They differ only in this: in the present situation the technical, practical conception of science as specialization can at least lay claim to frank and clear consistency, while the reactionary interpretation of science as a cultural value, now making its reappearance, seeks to conceal the impotence of the spirit behind an unconscious lie. The confusion of spiritlessness can even go so far as to lead the upholders of the technical, practical view of science to profess their belief in science as a cultural value; then the two understand each other perfectly in the same spiritlessness. We may choose to call the institution where the specialized sciences are grouped together for purposes of teaching and research a university, but this is no more than a name; the "university" has ceased to be a fundamental force for unity and responsibility. What I said here in 1929, in my inaugural address, is still true of the German university: "The scientific fields are still far apart. Their subjects are treated in fundamentally different ways. Today this hodgepodge of disciplines is held together only by the technical organization of the universities and faculties and preserves what meaning it has only through the practical aims of the different branches. The sciences have lost their roots in their essential ground." (*Was ist Metaphysik?* 1929, p. 8.) Science today in all its branches is a technical, practical business of gaining and transmitting information. An awakening of the spirit cannot take its departure from such science. It is itself in need of an awakening.

4. The last misinterpretation of the spirit is based on the above-mentioned falsifications which represent the spirit as intelligence, and intelligence as a serviceable tool which, along with its product, is situated in the realm of culture. In the end the spirit as utilitarian intelligence and the spirit as culture become holiday ornaments cultivated along with many other things. They are brought out and exhibited as a proof that there is *no* intention to combat culture or favor barbarism. In the beginning Russian Communism took a purely negative attitude but soon went over to propagandist tactics of this kind.

In opposition to this multiple misinterpretation of the spirit, we define the essence of the spirit briefly as follows

Ref. of Geist (Spirit)

(I shall quote from the address I delivered on the occasion of my appointment as rector, because of its succinct formulation): "Spirit is neither empty cleverness nor the irresponsible play of the wit, nor the boundless work of dismemberment carried on by the practical intelligence; much less is it world-reason; no, spirit is a fundamental, knowing resolve toward the essence of being." (Rektoratsrede, p. 13.) Spirit is the mobilization of the powers of the essent as such and as a whole. Where spirit prevails, the essent as such becomes always and at all times more essent. Thus the inquiry into the essent as such and as a whole, the asking of the question of being, is one of the essential and fundamental conditions for an awakening of the spirit and hence for an original world of historical being-there. It is indispensable if the peril of world darkening is to be forestalled and if our nation in the center of the Western world is to take on its historical mission. Here we can explain only in these broad outlines why the asking of the question of being is in itself through and through historical, and why, accordingly, our question as to whether being will remain a mere vapor for us or become the destiny of the West is anything but an exaggeration and a rhetorical figure.

But if our question about being has this essential and decisive character, we must above all take an absolutely serious view of *the fact* that gives the question its immediate necessity, the fact that for us being has become little more than a mere word and its meaning an evanescent vapor. This is not the kind of fact which merely confronts us as something alien and other, which we need merely note as an occurrence. It is a fact in which we stand. It is a state of our being-there. And by state, of course, I do not mean a quality that can be demonstrated only psychologically. Here state means our entire constitution, the way in which we ourselves are constituted in regard to being. Here we are not concerned with psychology but with our history in an essential respect. When we call it a "fact" that being for us is a mere word and vapor, we are speaking very provisionally. We are merely holding fast, establishing something which has not yet been thought through, for which we still have no locus, even if it looks as though this something were an occurrence among us, here and now, or "in" us, as we like to say.

One would like to integrate the individual fact that for us being remains no more than an empty word and an evanescent vapor with the more general fact that many words, and precisely the essential ones, are in the same situation; that the language in general is worn out and used up—an indispensable but masterless means of communication that may be used as one pleases, as indifferent as a means of public transport, as a street car which everyone rides in. Everyone speaks and writes away in the language, without hindrance and above all *without danger*. That is certainly true. And only a very few are capable of thinking through the full implications of this misrelation and unrelation of present-day being-there to language.

But the emptiness of the word "being," the total disappearance of its appellative force, is not merely a particular instance of the general exhaustion of language; rather, the destroyed relation to being as such is the actual reason for the general misrelation to language.   *LANGUAGE*

The organizations for the purification of the language and defense against its progressive barbarization are deserving of respect. But such efforts merely demonstrate all the more clearly that we no longer know what is at stake in language. Because the destiny of language is grounded in a nation's *relation* to *being*, the question of being will involve us deeply in the question of language. It is more than an outward accident that now, as we prepare to set forth, in all its implication, the fact of the evaporation of being, we find ourselves compelled to take linguistic considerations as our starting point.

2.

ON THE GRAMMAR
AND ETYMOLOGY OF
THE WORD "BEING"

If being has become no more for us than an empty word and an evanescent significance, we must try at least to capture wholly this remaining vestige of significance. With this in mind we ask first of all:

1. What sort of word is "being" in regard to its form?
2. What does linguistics tell us about the original meaning of this word?

To put it in learned terms: we shall inquire into 1) the grammar and 2) the etymology of the word "being."*

The grammar of words is not only and not primarily concerned with their literal and phonetic form. It takes these formal elements as indications of specific directions and differences of direction in the potential meanings of words and in the possible ways of employing them in a sentence or larger unit of discourse. The words he goes, we went, they have gone, go, going, to go are variations of the same word in accordance with definite directions of meaning. We know them from the titles in grammar books: present indicative, perfect, compound past, imperative, present participle, infinitive. But these terms ceased long ago to be anything more than technical instruments with the help of which we mechanically dissect language and set down rules. Precisely where a pristine feeling toward language still stirs, we sense the deadness of these

---

* On this section cf. Ernst Fraenkel, "Das Sein und seine Modalitäten" in *Lexis* (Studien zur Sprachphilosophie, Sprachgeschichte und Begriffsforschung), ed. Johannes Lohmann, 2 (1949), 149.

grammatical forms, these mere mechanisms. Language and linguistics have been caught fast in these rigid forms, as in a steel net. In the barren and spiritless doctrine of the schools, these formal concepts and terms of grammar have become totally uncomprehended and incomprehensible shells.

It is assuredly sound that instead of this our school children should learn something about Germanic prehistory and early history. But this will sink into the same barrenness unless we succeed in rebuilding the school's spiritual world from within and from out of the ground, i.e. in giving the school a spiritual, not a scientific, atmosphere. And here the first step must be a real revolution in the prevailing relation to language. But to this end we must revolutionize the teachers, and for this in turn the university must transform itself and learn to understand its task instead of puffing itself up with irrelevancies. It no longer even enters our heads that all these things we have known so long might be different, that these grammatical forms have not from all eternity stood there like absolutes, dissecting and regulating language as such, that quite on the contrary they grew out of a very definite interpretation of the Greek and Latin languages. And all this happened on the basis of the fact that language too is an essent, which like other essents can be made accessible and delimited in a definite way. Obviously the validity of such an undertaking and the way in which it was carried out depended on the fundamental view of being that guided it.

The determination of the essence of language, the very inquiry into it, are regulated at all times by the prevailing preconception about the essence of being and about essence itself. But essence and being express themselves in language. Here it is important to speak of this connection, because we are inquiring into the word "being." If, as is unavoidable at the start, we make use of traditional grammar and its forms in this grammatical designation of the word, we must, particularly in the present case, do so with the basic reservation that these grammatical forms are not adequate to our purpose. In the course of our investigations the example of a crucial grammatical form will demonstrate that this is so.

But this demonstration will soon go further, dispelling any appearance that our aim is to improve on grammar. Our aim, rather, is an essential clarification of the essence of being in respect to its essential involvement with the essence of language. This must be borne in mind in the following if we are not to mistake the linguistic and grammatical investigations for a sterile and irrelevant game. We shall inquire 1) into the grammar, 2) into the etymology of the word "being."

1. *The Grammar of the Word "Being"* ⟨ *Sein* ⟩*

What kind of word is "being" in respect to its word form? To "being" ⟨ das Sein ⟩ correspond going, falling, dreaming, etc. ⟨ das Gehen, das Fallen, das Träumen ⟩. These linguistic entities are nouns like bread, house, grass, thing. But we observe at once this difference: that we can easily reduce them to the verbs to go, to fall ⟨ gehen, fallen ⟩, etc., which does not seem to be possible with the other group. "House," to be sure, has the related form "to house": "he houses ⟨ dwells ⟩ in the forest." But the relation of grammar and meaning between "going" ⟨ das Gehen ⟩ and "to go" ⟨ gehen ⟩ is different from that between "the house" and "to house." On the other hand, there are word forms that correspond exactly to our first group (going, falling) and yet resemble "bread," "house" in word character and meaning. For example: "The ambassador gave an Essen" ⟨ dinner; infinitive essen, to eat ⟩. "He died of an incurable Leiden" ⟨ illness; infinitive leiden, to suffer ⟩. We no longer regard these words as pertaining to verbs. From the verb a substantive, a name, has developed, and this through a definite form of the verb which in Latin is called *modus infinitivus.*

We find the same relations in connection with our word Sein ⟨ being ⟩. This substantive goes back to the infinitive "sein" ⟨ to be ⟩, which belongs with the forms you are, he is, we were, they have been. "Being" as a substantive came out of the verb: the word "being" is a "verbal substantive." The mention of this grammatical form completes the linguistic

* For an understanding of this passage it is necessary to bear in mind that in German (as in most Western languages) the verbal noun "being" is supplied by an infinitive, Sein, and not, as in English, by a participial form. (R.M.)

designation of the word "being." These are well-known, self-evident things, and we are discussing them at great length. But it would be more cautious and correct to say that these linguistic, grammatical distinctions are worn-out conventions; for they are far from "self-evident." Consequently we must have a look at the grammatical forms in question (verb, substantive, substantivization of the verb, infinitive, participle).

It is easy to see that in the formation of the word form "das Sein" ⟨being⟩ the decisive preliminary form is the infinitive "sein" ⟨to be⟩. This form of the verb is transposed into the form of a substantive. Verb, infinitive, substantive are accordingly the three grammatical forms which determine the word character of our word "being" ⟨das Sein⟩. Hence it is first of all important to understand the significance of these grammatical forms. Two of the three, verb and substantive, are among those which were first recognized at the beginnings of Western grammar, and which today are still regarded as the fundamental forms of words and of grammar. Consequently our inquiry into the essence of the substantive and the verb takes us into the question of the essence of language. For the question as to whether the original form of the word was the noun (substantive) or the verb coincides with the question regarding the original character of discourse and speech in general. And this question contains within it the question of the origin of language. For the present we cannot go into this question directly, but must help ourselves with an expedient. We shall limit ourselves for the present to the grammatical form which provides a bridge to the formation of the verbal substantive, namely the infinitive (to go, to come, to fall, to sing, to hope, to be, etc.).

What does infinitive mean? The word is an abbreviation for *modus infinitivus,* the mode of unlimitedness, indeterminateness, namely in the manner in which a verb accomplishes and indicates its significative function and direction.

Like all other Latin grammatical terms, this term stems from the work of the Greek grammarians. Here again we run into the process of translation which we have mentioned in connection with the word *physis.* We need not go into the details here of how grammar arose among the Greeks, how it was taken over by the Romans and handed on to the Middle

Ages and the modern era. In regard to this history of grammar we know a good many details. So far there is no work that really penetrates this process, so fundamental to the establishment and formation of all Western spirit. We even lack an adequate formulation of the problems underlying such a study, which must inevitably be undertaken one day, remote as this whole matter may seem from current interests.

What gives this development its entire meaning is that Western grammar sprang from the reflection of the Greeks on the *Greek* language. For along with German the Greek language is (in regard to its possibilities for thought) at once the most powerful and most spiritual of all languages.

First of all it should be borne in mind that the crucial differentiation of the fundamental forms of words (noun and verb) in the Greek form of *onoma* and *rhēma* was worked out and first established in close connection with an exegesis and interpretation of being, which was to exert a determining influence on the whole West. The inner bond between these two processes has come down to us unimpaired and clearly formulated in Plato's *Sophist*. The terms *onoma* and *rhēma* were known to be sure before Plato. But at that time, as with Plato, they were taken as names covering the entire usage of words. *Onoma* meant the linguistic appellation in distinction to the named person or thing, and took in the utterance of a word which was later designated grammatically as *rhēma*. And *rhēma* in turn meant speech, discourse; *rhētōr* was the speaker, the orator, who employed not only verbs but also *onomata* in the restricted sense of substantive.

The fact that the two terms originally covered an equally broad field is important for the contention that we shall make further on, namely that the question, much discussed in linguistics, as to whether the noun or the verb is the original form of word is no authentic question. This pseudo question first grew up in the light of a developed grammar, and not from a contemplation of the essence of language as it was before the grammarians ripped it apart.

Subsequently the two terms *onoma* and *rhēma*, which originally designated all speech, narrowed in meaning and became terms for the two main classes of words. In *Sophist* (261 *e* ff.), Plato for the first time gave an interpretation and

explanation of this differentiation. He starts from the universal designation of the word's function. *Onoma* in the broader
sense is *dēlōma tēi phonēi peri tēn ousian,* revelation through
sound, in respect to and within the area of the being of the
essent.

In the realm of the essent a differentiation may be made
between *pragma* and *praxis. Pragmata* are the things with
which we have to do, with which we are always concerned.
Praxis is action and activity in the broadest sense, which also
includes *poiēsis.* Words are of twofold kind (*ditton genos*).
They are *dēlōma pragmatos* (*onoma*), revelation of things,
and *dēlōma praxeōs* (*rhēma*), revelation of an action. Where
a *plegma,* a *symplokē* (an interweaving of the two) occurs,
we have the *logos elachistos te kai prōtos,* the shortest (and
yet at the same time) first (authentic) discourse. But it was
Aristotle who first gave a clearer metaphysical interpretation of *logos* in the sense of statement. He differentiates
between *onoma* as *sēmantikon aneu chronon* and *rhēma* as
prossēmainon chronon (*De Interpretatione,* c. 2–4). This interpretation of the essence of *logos* was taken as a model in
the subsequent development of logic and grammar. And even
though grammar degenerated almost immediately into aca-
demicism, the subject itself retained its crucial importance. For
over a thousand years the works of the Greek and Latin
grammarians served as schoolbooks in the Western world.
We know that these periods were by no means feeble and
insignificant.

We are asking about the word form that the Romans called
infinitivus. In itself the negative form *modus infinitivus* points
to a *modus finitus,* a mode of limitation and determinateness
of verbal signification. Now what is the Greek prototype for
this distinction? What the Roman grammarians designated
by the colorless term *modus* was for the Greeks *enklisis,* in-
clination to the side. This word moves in the same direction
of meaning as another Greek word indicating grammatical
form. That is the word known to us from the Latin translation, *ptōsis, casus,* the case in respect to the inflection of the
noun. But originally *ptōsis* designated any kind of inflection
of the basic form (deviation, declension), not only in sub-
stantives but also in verbs. It was only after the difference

between these word forms had been more clearly worked out that their inflections were designated by different terms. The inflection of the noun is called *ptōsis* (*casus*); that of the verb *enklisis* (*declinatio*).

Now how did these two particular terms *ptōsis* and *enklisis* come into use in the study of language and its inflections? Language is obviously regarded as something that also is, as an essent among others. Hence the manner in which the Greeks understood the essent in its being was bound to make itself felt in their view and definition of language. Only on this basis can we understand these terms which, as mood and case, have long become threadbare and meaningless for us.

In this lecture we shall always be coming back to the Greeks' view of being, because this view, though totally banalized and unrecognized as Greek, is still the prevailing Western view. Since this is true not only in regard to the doctrines of philosophy but in the most common and everyday matters, we shall attempt, as we examine the Greek view of language, to characterize the first fundamentals of the Greek view of being.

This method is chosen intentionally. We hope to show by an example drawn from grammar that the determining Western experience, idea, and interpretation of language have grown out of a very definite understanding of being.

The words *ptōsis* and *enklisis* mean falling, tipping, inclining. This implies a deviation from standing upright and straight. But this erect standing-there, coming up ⟨ zum Stande kommen, coming to stand⟩ and enduring ⟨ im Stand bleiben, remaining in standing⟩ is what the Greeks understood by being. Yet what thus comes up and becomes intrinsically stable ⟨ständig⟩ encounters, freely and spontaneously, the necessity of its limit, *peras*. This limit is not something that comes to the essent from outside. Still less is it a deficiency in the sense of a harmful restriction. No, the hold that governs itself from out of the limit, the having-itself, wherein the enduring holds itself, is the being of the essent; it is what first makes the essent into an essent as differentiated from a nonessent. Coming to stand accordingly means: to achieve a limit for itself, to limit itself. Consequently a fundamental characteristic of the essent is *to telos*, which means not aim

or purpose but end. Here "end" is not meant in a negative
sense, as though there were something about it that did not
continue, that failed or ceased. End is ending in the sense of
fulfillment ⟨ Vollendung ⟩. Limit and end are that wherewith
the essent begins to *be*. It is on this basis that we must understand the supreme term that Aristotle used for being, *ente-*
lecheia—the holding (preserving)-itself-in-the-ending (limit).
What later philosophy, not to mention biology, made of the
term "entelechy" (cf. Leibniz) shows the full extent of the
degeneration from Greek thought. That which places itself
in its limit, completing it, and so stands, has form, *morphē*.
Form as the Greeks understood it derives its essence from an
emerging placing-itself-in-the-limit.

But from the viewpoint of the beholder that which stands-
there-in-itself becomes that which re-presents itself, which
presents itself in what it looks like. The Greeks call the appearance of a thing *eidos* or *idea*. Initially *eidos* included a
resonance of what we too have in mind when we say: the
thing has a face, it can let itself be seen, it stands. The thing
"sits." It rests in the manifestation, i.e. emergence, of its essence. But all the definitions of being that we shall now list
are grounded in, and are held together by, that wherein the
Greeks unquestionably experienced the meaning of being,
and which they called *ousia*, or more fully *parousia*. The usual,
unthinking translation of this word as "substance" misses its
meaning completely. For *parousia* we have in German a corresponding term—An-wesen ⟨ presence ⟩, which also designates
an estate or homestead, standing in itself or self-enclosed. In
Aristotle's time *ousia* was used both in this sense and in the
sense of the fundamental term of philosophy. Something is
present to us. It stands steadily by itself and thus manifests
itself. It is. For the Greeks "being" basically meant this standing presence.

But Greek philosophy never returned to this ground of
being and to what it implies. It remained on the surface of
that which is present and sought to examine it in the determinations we have cited.

We now have a better understanding of the Greek view of
being mentioned above in our explanation of the term metaphysics, namely the experience of being as *physis*. As we said,

the later concepts of "nature" must be set aside: *physis* means the emerging and arising, the spontaneous unfolding that lingers. In this power rest and motion are opened out of original unity. This power is the overpowering presence that is not yet mastered ⟨ bewältigt ⟩ in thought, wherein that which is present manifests itself as an essent. But this power first issues from concealment, i.e. in Greek: *alētheia* (unconcealment) when the power accomplishes itself as a world.

It is through world that the essent first becomes essent.

Heraclitus says (Fragment 53): "Conflict is for all (that is present) the creator that causes to emerge, but (also) for all the dominant preserver. For it makes some to appear as gods, others as men; it creates (shows) some as slaves, others as freemen."*

The *polemos* named here is a conflict that prevailed prior to everything divine and human, not a war in the human sense. This conflict, as Heraclitus thought it, first caused the realm of being to separate into opposites; it first gave rise to position and order and rank. In such separation cleavages, intervals, distances, and joints opened. In the conflict ⟨ Auseinandersetzung, setting-apart ⟩ a world comes into being. (Conflict does not split, much less destroy unity. It constitutes unity, it is a binding-together, *logos*. *Polemos* and *logos* are the same.)

The struggle meant here is the original struggle, for it gives rise to the contenders as such; it is not a mere assault on something already there. It is this conflict that first projects and develops what had hitherto been unheard of, unsaid and unthought. The battle is then sustained by the creators, poets, thinkers, statesmen. Against the overwhelming chaos they set the barrier of their work, and in their work they capture the world thus opened up. It is with these works that the elemental power, the *physis* first comes to stand. Only now does the essent become essent as such. This world-building is history in the authentic sense. Not only does conflict as such give rise to ⟨ ent-stehen lassen ⟩ the essent; it also preserves the essent in its permanence ⟨ Ständigkeit ⟩. Where struggle

---

* πόλεμος πάντων μὲν πατήρ ἐστι, πάντων δὲ βασιλεύς, καὶ τοὺς μὲν θεοὺς ἔδειξε τοὺς δὲ ἀνθρώπους, τοὺς μὲν δούλους ἐποίησε τοὺς δὲ ἐλευθέρους.

ceases, the essent does not vanish, but the world turns away. The essent is no longer asserted (i.e. preserved as such). Now it is merely found ready-made; it is datum. The end result is no longer that which is impressed into limits (i.e. placed in its form); it is merely finished and as such available to every-one, already-there, no longer embodying any world—now man does as he pleases with what is available. The essent becomes an object, either to be beheld (view, image) or to be acted upon (product and calculation). The original world-making power, *physis*, degenerates into a prototype to be copied and imitated. Nature becomes a special field, differentiated from art and everything that can be fashioned according to plan. The original emergence and standing of energies, the *phaines-thai*, or appearance in the great sense of a world epiphany, becomes a visibility of things that are already-there and can be pointed out. The eye, the vision, which originally pro-jected the project into potency, becomes a mere looking at or looking over or gaping at. Vision has degenerated into mere optics (Schopenhauer's "world eye"—pure cognition . . .).

True, there are still essents. There are more of them, and they make more of a stir than ever. But being has gone out of them. The essent has been made into an "object" of end-less and variegated busy-ness, and only thereby has it re-tained an appearance of its permanence.

When the creators vanish from the nation, when they are barely tolerated as an irrelevant curiosity, an ornament, as eccentrics having nothing to do with real life; when authen-tic conflict ceases, converted into mere polemics, into the machinations and intrigues of man within the realm of the given, then the decline has set in. For even if an epoch still strives to maintain the inherited level and dignity of its being-there, the level falls. It can be maintained only if it is at all times creatively transcended.

"Being" meant for the Greeks: permanence in a twofold sense:

1. standing-in-itself ⟨ In-sich-stehen ⟩ in the sense of aris-ing ⟨ Ent-stehen, standing-out-of ⟩ (*physis*),

2. but, as such, "permanent" ⟨ ständig ⟩, i.e. enduring (*ousia*).

Nonbeing means accordingly to depart from such generated permanence: *existasthai,* "existence," "to exist," meant for the Greeks precisely nonbeing. The thoughtless habit of using the words "existence" and "exist" as designations for being is one more indication of our estrangement both from being and from a radical, forceful, and definite exegesis of being.

Ptōsis, enklisis mean to fall, to incline, i.e. to depart and deviate from permanent standing. We raise the question: why did just these two terms come into use in linguistics? The significance of the words *ptōsis–enklisis* presupposes the notion of a standing upright. As we have said, the Greeks viewed language as something essent, hence in line with their understanding of being. Essent is that which is permanent and represents itself as such, that which appears and manifests itself primarily to vision. In a certain broad sense the Greeks looked on language from a visual point of view, that is, starting from the written language. It is in writing that the spoken language comes to stand. Language is, i.e. it stands in the written image of the word, in the written signs, the letters, *grammata.* Consequently grammar represents language in being. But through the flow of speech language seeps away into the impermanent. Thus, down to our own time, language has been interpreted grammatically. But the Greeks also knew of the phonetic character of language, the *phonē.* They established rhetoric and poetics. (But all this did not in itself lead to an appropriate definition of the essence of language.)

The crucial view of language remains the grammatical view. Among the words and their forms it finds some that are deviations from, modulations of, fundamental forms. The fundamental position of the noun (the substantive) is the nominative singular: e.g. *ho kyklos,* the circle. The fundamental position of the verb is the first person singular of the present indicative; e.g. *legō,* I say. The infinitive on the other hand is a special mode of the verb, an *enklisis.* Of what kind? This may best be determined by an example. One form of *legō* is *lexainto.* "They (the men in question) might be said to be and called"—traitors for example. On close scrutiny we find that this inflectional form discloses a different person (the third), another number (not singular but plural), another voice (passive instead of active), another tense (aorist instead of present), another mood in the restricted sense (not indicative but optative). What is named in the word is not invoked as really present but represented as only potentially in being.

The inflected form discloses all this as part of its meaning and causes it to be immediately understood. To disclose something different along with the fundamental meaning, to cause it to arise and be seen: therein lies the power of the *enklisis*, in which the erect word leans to one side. It is therefore called *enklisis paremphatikos*. The characteristic *paremphaino* stems authentically from the fundamental relation of the Greeks to the essent as the standing, the permanent.

Plato (*Timaeus*, 50 e) uses the word in an important context. In this passage he inquires about the becoming of that which becomes. To become means "to come to being." Plato differentiates three classes: 1) *to gignomen*, that which becomes; 2) *to en hōi gignetai*, that *wherein* it becomes, the medium in which a thing in process of becoming forms itself and out of which, once become, it emerges; 3) *to hothen aphomoioumenon*, that whence that which becomes derives the standard of resemblance; for everything in process of becoming, that becomes something, anticipates what it is going to become and takes it as a model.

For clarification of the meaning of *paremphaino* let us consider what has been said under 2). That wherein something becomes refers to what we call "space." The Greeks had no word for "space." This is no accident; for they experienced the spatial on the basis not of extension but of place (*topos*); they experienced it as *chōra*, which signifies neither place nor space but that which is occupied by what stands there. The place belongs to the thing itself. Each of all the various things has its place. That which becomes is placed in this local "space" and emerges from it. But in order that this should be possible, "space" must be free from all the modes of appearance that it might derive from anywhere. For if it were similar to any of the modes of appearance that enter into it, it would, in receiving forms of antithetical or totally different essence, manifest its own appearance and so produce a poor realization of the model.* That wherein the things in process of becoming are placed must precisely not present an aspect and appearance of its own. (The reference to the passage in *Timaeus* is intended not only to clarify the link between the *paremphainon* and the *on*, between also-appearing and being as permanence, but at the same time to suggest that the transformation of the barely apprehended essence of place (*topos*) and of *chōra* into a "space" defined by extension was initiated by the Platonic philosophy, i.e. in the interpretation of being as *idea*. Might *chōra* not mean: that which abstracts itself from every particular, that which withdraws, and in such a way precisely admits and "makes place" for something else?) Let us return to the form *lexainto*. It manifests a *poikilia* of directions of meaning. For this reason it is called *enklisis paremphatikos*, a deviation which *is* able to manifest person, number, tense, voice, mood along with its basic meaning. This is grounded in the fact that the word as such *is* a word, insofar as it causes to appear (*dēloun*). If to the form *lexainto* we compare the form *legein*, the infinitive, we find here too an inflection, an *enklisis* over against the basic form *legō*, but one in which person, number, mood are *not* manifested. Here the *enklisis* and its function of manifesting reveal a deficiency. Accordingly, this form is called *enklisis a-paremphatikos*. In Latin the term corresponding to this negative term is *modus infinitivus*. The meaning of the infinitive form is not limited and cut to order in the respects we have mentioned, according to person, number, etc. The Latin translation of *a-paremphatikos* by *in-finitivus* deserves our attention. The original Greek with its reference to the appearance and coming-to-appear of what stands erect or inclines has vanished. Now the determining factor is the formal concept of limitation.

But of course the infinitive occurs, and particularly in Greek, in the passive and middle voice, and in the present, perfect, and future; it manifests at least voice and tense. This has raised various controversies about the infinitive, which

---

* *Timaeus* 50 e: ἄμορφον ὄν ἐκείνον ἀπασῶν τῶν ἰδεῶν ὅσας μέλλοι δέχεσθαί ποθεν. ὅμοιον γὰρ ὄν τῶν ἐπεισιόντων τινὶ τὰ τῆς ἐναντίας τά τε τῆς παράπαν ἄλλης φύσεως ὁπότ' ἔλθοι δεχόμενον κακῶς ἂν ἀφομοιοῖ τὴν αὐτοῦ παρεμφαῖνον ὄψιν.

we shall not take up here. But there is one point that should
be clarified for our purposes. The infinitive form *legein*, to
say, can be understood in such a way that we no longer think
of voice and tense but only of what the verb as such intends
and manifests. In this respect the original Greek term is particularly apt. According to the Latin term the infinitive is
a form that may be said to cut off the meaning from all definite relations. The meaning is drawn out (ab-stracted) from
all the particular relationships. In this abstraction the infinitive yields only what is represented by the word as such.
Hence present-day grammarians say that the infinitive is the
"abstract verbal concept." It comprehends and formulates the
meaning only in a general sense. It designates only this general meaning. In our language the infinitive is the form by
which one refers to a verb. And there is a lack, a deficiency
in the form and mode of meaning of the infinitive. The infinitive *no longer* manifests what the verb otherwise reveals.

And indeed the infinitive is a late, in fact the latest, form
in the order of linguistic development. This may be demonstrated by the example of the infinitive of the Greek word
whose questionable character led to our discussion. "Being"
⟨i.e. to be⟩ is in Greek *einai*. We know that a literary language develops from dialects with their original local and
historical roots. The language of Homer is a mixture of different dialects which preserve the earlier form of the language. It is in the formation of the infinitive that the Greek
dialects are most divergent, and for this reason linguists have
come to use divergent infinitives as the chief criterion "by
which to differentiate and group the dialects." (See Wacker-
nagel, *Vorlesungen über Syntax*, 1, 257 f.)

To be is in Attic *einai*, in Arcadien *ēnai*, in Lesbian *emmenai*, in Doric *ēmen*. In Latin it is *esse*, in Oscan *ezum*, in
Umbrian *erom*. In both languages the *modi finiti* were already
stabilized and uniform at a time when the *enklisis aparem-
phatikos* still preserved its dialectical peculiarities and fluc-
tuations. We consider this circumstance as an indication that
the infinitive carries a privileged significance in language as
a whole. The question remains whether the power of the infinitive forms to endure stems from the fact that the infinitive
is an abstract and late verb form or from the fact that it

names something which underlies all the inflections of the verb. On the other hand, there is justification in the warning that we should be on our guard against the infinitive form, since from a grammatical point of view it is the form that communicates the least of the verb's meaning.

But we have not yet fully elucidated the word form under discussion, namely the form in which we customarily speak of "being." We say "das Sein." This form arises when by prefacing it with an article we transform the abstract infinitive into a substantive: *to einai*. The article was originally a demonstrative pronoun. It signifies that the object indicated stands as it were for itself, and is. This function of demonstration and indication always plays an eminent role in language. If we say only "sein," what is named is already indefinite enough. But the transformation of the infinitive into a verbal substantive further stabilizes as it were the emptiness that already resided in the infinitive; "sein" is set down like a stable object. The substantive "Sein" ⟨being⟩ implies that what has thus been named itself "is." Now "being" itself becomes something that "is," though manifestly only essents are and not being in addition. But if being itself were something essent in an essent, then we should have to find it, particularly as the essentness ⟨das Seiendsein⟩ of an essent confronts us even when we do not definitely apprehend its particular properties.

Can it now surprise us that "being" should be so empty a word when the very word form is based on an emptying and an apparent stabilization of emptiness? Let this word "being" be a warning to us. Let us not be lured into the emptiest of all forms, the verbal substantive. And let us not get caught in the abstraction of the infinitive "sein." If we wish to penetrate to "being" from language, let us stick to the forms I am, thou art, he, she, it is, we are, etc., I was, we were, they have been, etc. But this does not make our understanding of what "being" means in this connection, and wherein its essence consists, one bit plainer! On the contrary! Let us make the experiment.

We say "I am." Each man can assert the being here intended only for himself: my being. Wherein does it consist, and where does it reside? Seemingly this is what should be easiest for us to bring to light, for to no essent are we so close as to what we ourselves are. Everything else "is" no less even if we ourselves are not. Apparently we cannot be so close to any other essent as to the essent that we ourselves are. Actually we cannot even say that we are close to the essent that we ourselves are, since we itself are it. And yet the truth is that everyone is remotest from himself, as remote as the I from the you in "you are."

But today it is the we that counts. Now is the "time of the we," not of the I. We are. What being are we naming in this sentence? We say also: the windows are, the stones are. We —are. Does this statement mean that a plurality of I's is present? And what about the "I was" and "we were," what about being in the past? Has it gone away from us? Or *are* we exactly what we were? Are we not becoming just exactly what we *are?*

Scrutiny of the definite verbal forms of "to be" brings the opposite of a clarification of being. Moreover, it leads to a new difficulty. Let us compare the infinitive "to say" and the base form "I say" with the infinitive "to be" and the base form "I am." "Be" and "am" ⟨ "sein" and "bin" ⟩ prove to be different words in respect to their root. Different from both in turn are the "was" and "been" ⟨ "war" and "gewesen" ⟩ of the past forms. This brings us to the question of the different roots of the word "being."

2. The Etymology of the Word "Being"

First of all we must briefly report what is known to the science of linguistics about the roots that occur in the inflections of the verb "sein." Present knowledge of the subject is by no means definitive; not so much because new facts may come to light, as because it is to be expected that those already known will be examined with new eyes and a more authentic questioning. The entire range of the inflections of the verb "sein" is determined by three different stems.

The first two stems to be named are Indo-European and also occur in the Greek and Latin words for "being."

1. The oldest, the actual radical word is *es*, Sanskrit *asus*,

life, the living, that which from out of itself stands and which moves and rests in itself: the self-standing ⟨ Eigenständig ⟩. To this radical belong in Sanskrit the verbal formations *esmi, esi, esti, asmi,* to which correspond the Greek *eimi* and *einai,* the Latin *esum* and *esse. Sunt,* sind, and sein belong together. It is noteworthy that the "ist" has maintained itself in all Germanic languages from the very start (*estin, est . . .*).

2. The other Indo-European radical is *bhu, bheu.* To it belong the Greek *phuō,* to emerge, to be powerful, of itself to come to stand and remain standing. Up until now this *bhu* has been interpreted according to the usual superficial view of *physis* and *phyein* as nature and "to grow." A more fundamental exegesis, stemming from preoccupation with the beginning of Greek philosophy, shows the "growing" to be an "emerging," which in turn is defined by presence and appearance. Recently the root *phy-* has been connected with *pha-phainesthai. Physis* would then be that which emerges into the light, *phyein* would mean to shine, to give light and therefore to appear. (See *Zeitschrift für vergleichende Sprachforschung,* Vol. 59.)

From this stem come the Latin perfect *fui, fuo;* similarly our German "bin," "bist," wir "birn," ihr "birt" (which died out in the fourteenth century). The imperative "bis" ("bis mein Weib, be my wife") survived longer.

3. The third stem occurs only in the inflection of the Germanic verb "sein": *wes;* Sanskrit: *vasami;* Germanic: *wesan,* to dwell, to sojourn; to *ves* belong: ϝ*estia,* ϝ*asti, Vesta, vestibulum.* The German forms resulting from this stem are "gewesen," was, war, es west, wesen. The participle "wesend" is still preserved in an-wesend ⟨ present ⟩ and ab-wesend ⟨ absent ⟩. The substantive "Wesen" did not originally mean "whatness," quiddity, but enduring as presence, presence and absence. The *sens* in the Latin *prae-sens* and *ab-sens* has been lost. Does *Dii consentes* mean the gods who are present together?

From the three stems we derive the three initial concrete meanings: to live, to emerge, to linger or endure. These are established by linguistics, which also establishes that these initial meanings are extinct today, that only an "abstract" meaning "to be" has been preserved. But here a crucial ques-

tion arises: how and wherein do the three stems accord?
What sustains and guides the saga ⟨Sage⟩ of being? What
is the content of our use of the word "being"—after all its linguistic modulations? Are our use of the word and our understanding of being the same or are they not? How does the
distinction between being and the essent dwell in the enun-
ciation ⟨Sage⟩ of being? Valuable as the findings of linguistics are, they do not provide an answer. For it is only after
these facts are established that the *questioning* can begin.

We must ask a whole series of questions:

1. What sort of "abstraction" was at work in the formation
of the word "sein"?

2. May we, in the first place, speak of abstraction in this
connection?

3. What then is the abstract meaning that remains?

4. Can we explain the process that here opens up to us,
the process by which different meanings, hence experiences,
grow together to form the inflections of *one* verb, and not
just any verb but a very particular one, simply by saying that
something has been lost? Nothing arises through mere loss,
and least of all something which in the unity of its meaning
unites and merges elements that were originally different.

5. What fundamental meaning can have guided the mixture that has here taken place?

6. What orientation of meaning carries through, unblurred
by this mixture?

7. Ordinarily the history of the word "sein" is considered
on a level with that of other words whose etymology is being
investigated. But should we not except it from this equivalence, particularly if we bear in mind that even the root
meanings (live, emerge, dwell) invoke something more than
indifferent particulars in the sphere of the sayable, and by
naming it first disclose it?

8. Can the meaning of being, which on the basis of a
purely logical, grammatical interpretation strikes us as "abstract" and hence derived, be inherently whole and fundamental?

9. Can this be shown through language if we take a sufficiently basic view of it?

As the fundamental question of metaphysics we ask "Why are there essents rather than nothing?" This fundamental question, if we go deeply enough into its origins, implies the preliminary question "How does it stand with being?"

What do we mean by the words "to be," "being"? In attempting to answer, we immediately run into difficulties. We reach into the intangible. Yet we are unremittingly affected by the essent, we live in a continuous relation to the essent, and we know of ourselves "as essents."

"Being" remains barely a sound to us, a threadbare appellation. If nothing more is left to us, we must seek at least to grasp this last vestige of a possession. Therefore we ask "How does it stand with the *word 'being'* ⟨ das Sein ⟩?"

We have answered this question in two ways which have led us into the grammar and the etymology of the word. Let us sum up the results of this twofold discussion of the word "das Sein."

1. Grammatical investigation of the word form shows that in the infinitive the definite meanings of the word no longer make themselves felt; they are effaced. Substantivization completely stabilizes and objectifies this effacement. The word becomes a name for something indeterminate.

2. Etymological investigation of the word's meaning has shown that in respect to meaning what we have long called by the name of "das Sein" is a compromise and mixture of three different radical meanings. None of these reaches up independently to determine the meaning of the word. Mixture and effacement go hand in hand. In the combination of these two processes we find an adequate explanation of the fact from which we started, that the word "being" is empty and its meaning a vapor.

3

THE QUESTION OF
THE ESSENCE OF BEING

We have undertaken a study of the word "being" in order to penetrate the fact under discussion and so to assign it
its proper place. We do not mean to accept this fact blindly,
as we accept the fact that there are dogs and cats. We intend to form an opinion of the fact itself. And this we intend
to do even at the risk that this intention may give an impression of stubbornness, and be set down as a forlorn unworldli-
ness which takes the irrelevant and unreal for reality and
entangles itself in the dissection of mere words. We wish to
illuminate the fact. The result of our efforts is the observation that in the process of its development language forms
"infinitives," e.g. "sein," and that in the course of time language has produced a blunted, indefinite meaning of this
word. This happens to *be* so. Instead of gaining an elucidation of the fact, we have merely set another fact, pertaining
to the history of language, beside it or behind it.

If we now start again with these facts of the history of language and ask why they are as they are, what we perhaps
may still cite as a ground of explanation becomes not clearer
but more obscure. Then the fact that things stand as they
do with the word "being" really congeals into its inexorable
facticity. But this happened long ago. Those who follow the
usual method in philosophy are indeed invoking this fact when
they say at the very outset: the word "being" has the emptiest
and therefore most comprehensive meaning. What is thought
in connection with this word is consequently the supreme

generic concept, the genus. One can still barely detect the "ens in genere" as the old ontology puts it, but just as certainly there is nothing further to be sought in that direction. To attach the crucial question of metaphysics to this empty word "being" is to bring everything into confusion. Here there is only the one possibility, to recognize the emptiness of the word and let it go at that. This we may now apparently do with a clear conscience; and all the more so since the fact is explained historically by the history of language.

Let us then get away from the empty schema of this word "being." But where to? The answer cannot be difficult. At most we may wonder why we have dwelt so long, and in such detail, on the word "being." Away from the empty, universal word "being"; let us concern ourselves with the particulars of the different realms of the essent itself. For this undertaking we have all sorts of things at our disposal. The immediately tangible things, all the things that are constantly at hand, tools, vehicles, etc. If these particular essents strike us as too commonplace, not refined and soulful enough for "metaphysics," we can restrict ourselves to the nature around us, the land, the sea, the mountains, rivers, woods, and to the particulars therein, the trees, birds, insects, grasses, and stones. If we are looking for a large, impressive essent, the earth is close at hand. Essent in the same way as the nearest mountaintop is the moon that is rising back there, or a planet. Essent is the swarming crowd of people in a busy street. Essent are we ourselves. Essent are the Japanese. Essent are Bach's fugues. Essent is the Strassburg cathedral. Essent are Hölderlin's hymns. Essent are criminals. Essent are the lunatics in the lunatic asylum.

Everywhere essents to our heart's content. But how do we know that each one of all these things that we cite and list with so much assurance is an essent? The question sounds absurd, for any normal individual can establish infallibly that this essent *is*. Yes, to be sure. [Nor is it even necessary for us to use such words, alien to our everyday speech, as "essents" and the "essent."] And actually it does not enter our heads at this moment to doubt *that* all these essents really are, basing our doubts on the supposedly scientific observation that what we experience is only our sensations and that we can never escape our body, to which all the things we have named remain related. As a matter of fact we should like to remark in advance that such considerations, with which people so easily give themselves critical and superior airs, are thoroughly uncritical.

Meanwhile we shall simply *let* the essent *be*, as it surrounds us and assails us, as it inspires us or dejects us, in our everyday lives as well as in great hours and moments. We shall let all the essent *be*, just as it is. But if we thus hold to the course of our historical being-there, without soul searching and as though taking it for granted; if in every case we let the essent be the essent that it *is*, then we must know what "is" and "being" mean.

But how are we to determine whether an essent, presumed to be at some place and time, is or is not, if we cannot clearly differentiate in advance between being and nonbeing? How are we to make this crucial distinction unless we definitely know the meaning of what we are differentiating: namely nonbeing and being. How can each and every essent be an essent for us unless we understand "being" and "nonbeing" beforehand?

But essents are always confronting us. We differentiate between their being-so and being-otherwise, we make judgments regarding being and nonbeing. Accordingly we know clearly what "being" means. Then it is a superficial figure of speech and an error to say that this word is empty and indeterminate.

Such considerations bring us into an extremely contradictory situation. At the start we established that the word "being" tells us nothing definite. We did not make up our minds to this in advance; no, we found out, and we still find, that "being" has a vague and indeterminate meaning. Yet on the other hand the investigation we have just carried through convinces us that we clearly and surely distinguish "being" from nonbeing.

If we are to orient ourselves in this situation, we must bear in mind the following: It may indeed be doubtful whether a particular essent, somewhere or at some time, is or is not. We can make a mistake, for example as to whether that window there, which is after all an essent, *is* or *is not* closed. But even in order that the doubt may arise, the definite distinction between being and nonbeing must be present in our minds. In this case we do not doubt that being is different from nonbeing.

Thus the word "being" is indefinite in meaning and yet we understand it definitely. "Being" proves to be totally indeterminate and at the same time highly determinate. From the standpoint of the usual logic we have here an obvious contradiction. Something that contradicts itself cannot be. There is no such thing as a square circle. And yet we have this contradiction: determinate, wholly indeterminate being. If we decline to delude ourselves, and if we have a moment's time to spare amid all the activities and diversions of the day, we find ourselves standing in the very middle of this contradiction. And this "stand" of ours is more real than just about anything else that we call real; it is more real than dogs and cats, automobiles and newspapers.

Suddenly the fact that being is an empty word for us takes on an entirely different face. We begin to suspect that the word may not be as empty as alleged. If we reflect more closely on the word, it ultimately turns out that despite all the blur and mixture and universality of its meaning we mean something definite by it. This definiteness is so definite and unique in its kind that we must even say this:

The being which belongs to every essent whatsoever, and which is thus dispersed among all that is most current and familiar, is more unique than all else.

Everything else, each and every essent, even if it is unique, can be compared with other things. Its determinability is increased by these possibilities of comparison. By virtue of them it is in many respects indeterminate. Being, however, can be compared with nothing else. Over against being, the only other is nothing. And here there is no comparison. If being thus represents what is most unique and determinate, the word "being" cannot be empty. And in truth it never is empty. We may easily convince ourselves of this by a comparison. When we perceive the word "being," either hearing it as a phonetic unit or seeing it as a written sign, it immediately gives itself as something other than the succession of sounds and letters "abracadabra." This too is a succession of sounds, but we say at once that it is meaningless, though it may have its meaning as a magic formula. But "being" is not meaningless in this way. Similarly "being," written and seen, is at once different from "kzomil." This too is a sequence of letters but in connection with this sequence we cannot think anything. There is no such thing as an empty word; at most a word is worn out, though still filled with meaning. The name "being" retains its appellative force. "Away from this empty word 'being'; go to the particular essents," proves to be not only a hasty but also a highly questionable counsel. Let us once more think the whole matter through with the help of an example which, to be sure, like every example that we cite in dealing with this question, can never clarify the whole matter in its full scope and therefore must be taken with certain reservations.

By way of an example, we substitute for the universal concept "being" the universal concept "tree." If we wish now to say and define what the essence of tree is, we turn away from the universal concept to the particular species of tree and the particular specimens of these species. This method is so self-evident that we almost hesitate to mention it. Yet the matter is not as simple as all that. How are we going to find our famous particulars, the individual trees *as such, as* trees; how shall we be able even to *look for* trees, unless the representation of what a tree in general is shines before us? If this universal representation "tree" were so utterly indeterminate and blurred as to give us no certain indication for seeking and finding, we might perfectly well turn up automobiles or rabbits as our determinate particulars, as examples for tree. Even though it may be true that in order to determine the essence "tree" in every respect, we must pass through the particular, it remains at least equally true that the elucidation of essence and richness of essence is contingent on the radicalness with which we represent and know the universal essence "tree," which in this case means the essence "plant," which in turn means the essence "living things" and "life." Unless we are guided by a developed knowledge of tree-ness, which is manifestly determined from out of itself and its essential ground, we can look over thousands and thousands of trees in vain—we shall not see the tree for the trees.

Now, precisely in regard to "being," one might reply that since it is the most universal of concepts our representation cannot rise from it to anything higher. In dealing with this supreme and most universal concept reference to what is subsumed "under" it not only is advisable but is the only hope of overcoming its emptiness.

Striking as this argument may seem, it is false. Here let us give two reasons:

1. It is in general open to question whether the universality of being is a universality of genus. Aristotle already suspected this. Consequently it remains questionable whether an individual being can ever be regarded as an example of being, in the same way that oak is an example of "tree as such." It is doubtful whether the modes of being (being as nature, being as history) represent "species" in the "genus" being.

2. The word "being" is indeed a universal name and seemingly a word among others. But this appearance is deceptive. The name and what it names are unique. For this reason any illustration by examples is a distortion: in this case every example proves not too much but too little. We have pointed out above that we must know in advance what "tree" means in order to be able to seek and find the particulars: the tree species and the individual trees. This is still truer of being. Supreme and incomparable is the necessity that we understand the word "being" beforehand. Hence it does not follow from the "universality" of "being" in relation to all essents that we must hasten to turn away from it, toward the particular; no, what follows is just the opposite, that we should persevere with being and raise the uniqueness of this name and what it names to the level of knowledge.

Over against the fact that the meaning of the word "being" remains an indeterminate vapor for us, the fact that we understand being and differentiate it with certainty from nonbeing is not just another, second fact; rather, the two belong together, they are one. Meanwhile this one has altogether lost the character of a fact for us. We do not find it *also* given among many other facts. Instead we begin to suspect that some process is at work in what we have hitherto regarded as a mere fact. And the nature of this process excepts it from other "occurrences."

But before we resume our endeavor to find out what process is at work in this fact, let us make one last attempt to take it as something familiar and indifferent. Let us assume that this fact does not exist. Let us suppose that this indeterminate meaning of being does not exist and that we also do not understand what this meaning means. What then? Would there merely be a noun and a verb less in our language? No. *There would be no language at all.* No essent *as such* would disclose itself in words, it would no longer be possible to invoke it and speak about it in words. For to speak of an essent as such includes: to understand it in advance as an essent, that is, to understand its being. Assuming that we did not understand being at all, assuming that the word "being" did not even have its vaporous meaning, there would not be a single word. We ourselves could never be *speakers*. Altogether we could not be as we are. For to be a man is to speak. Man says yes and no only because in his profound essence he is a speaker, *the* speaker. That is his distinction and at the same time his burden. It distinguishes him from stones, plants, animals, but also from the gods. Even if we had a thousand eyes and a thousand ears, a thousand hands and many other senses and organs, if our essence did not include the power of language, all essents would be closed to us, the essent that we ourselves are no less than the essent that we are not.

A review of our discussion up to this point discloses the following situation: by setting down as a fact this (hitherto nameless) assumption, i.e. that being is for us an empty word of vaporous meaning, we depreciated it and deprived it of its proper rank. For our being-there, indeed, our understanding of being, even though indefinite, has the highest rank, since therein is revealed a power in which the essential possibility of our being-there is grounded. This is not a fact among other facts but something to which the highest rank should be accorded, provided that our being-there, which is always a historical being-there, does not remain indifferent to us. Yet even in order that our being-there should remain for us an indifferent essent, we should have to understand being. Without this understanding we should not even be able to say no to our being-there.

It is only by appreciating this pre-eminence of the understanding of being that we preserve it in its rank. In what way can we appreciate this rank, maintain it in its dignity? This we cannot decide arbitrarily.

Because the understanding of being resides first and foremost in a vague, indefinite meaning, and yet remains certain and definite; because, accordingly, the understanding of being, with all its rank, remains obscure, confused, and hidden, it must be elucidated, disentangled, and torn from its concealment. This can be done only if we inquire *about* this understanding of being which we at first accepted as a mere fact—if we put it in question.

Questioning is the authentic and proper and only way of appreciating what by its supreme rank holds our existence in its power. Hence no question is more worthy of being asked than that of our understanding of being, unless it be that of being itself. The more authentic our questioning, the more immediately and steadfastly we dwell on the most questionable of all questions, namely the circumstance that we understand being quite indefinitely and yet with supreme definiteness.

We understand the word "being" and with it all its inflections, even though it looks as though this understanding remained indefinite. Regarding what we understand, regarding what in some way *opens* itself to us in understanding, we say: it has a meaning. Insofar as it is in any way understood, being has a meaning. To experience and understand being as the most worthy of problems, to inquire specially after being, means then nothing other than to ask after the meaning of being.

In *Sein und Zeit* the question of the meaning of being is raised and developed *as a question* for the first time in the history of philosophy. It is also stated and explained in detail what is meant by meaning (namely the disclosure of being, not only of the essent as such; see *Sein und Zeit*, §§ 32, 44, 65).

Why may we no longer call what we have just mentioned a fact? Why was this term misleading from the very start? Because this circumstance that we understand being does not just occur among other circumstances in our lives, as, for example, the circumstance that we possess ear lobes of such and such form. Instead of these ear lobes, some other structure might serve as part of our hearing organ. That we understand being is not only real; it is also necessary. Without such a disclosure of being we could not be "the human race." To be sure, it is not absolutely necessary that we should be. There is the pure possibility that man might not be at all. After all there was a time when man was not. But strictly speaking we cannot say: There was a time when man *was* not. At all *times* man was and is and will be, because time produces itself only insofar as man is. There is no time when man was not, not because man was from all eternity and will be for all eternity but because time is not eternity and time fashions itself into a time only as a human, historical being-there. But a necessary condition for his being-there is that he understand being. Insofar as this is necessary, man is historically real. Therefore we understand being and not only, as it may appear at first sight, in the manner of the vague meaning of the word. No, the determinateness with which we understand the indeterminate meaning can be unambiguously delimited, and not after the fact, but as a determinateness which, unbeknownst to us, governs us from out of our very foundations. In order to show this, we start again from the word "being." But here it should be recalled that, in line with the basic metaphysical question set forth in the beginning, we take the word in the widest sense: it finds its limit only at nothing. Everything that is not simply nothing *is*, and for us even nothing "belongs" to "being."

In the present discussion we have taken a decisive step. In a lecture everything depends on such steps. Occasional questions that have been submitted to me about this lecture have shown me over and over again that most people listen in the wrong direction and become entangled in details. True, even in lectures on the special sciences, it is the context that counts. But for the sciences the context is determined directly by the object, which for the sciences is always in some way present. For philosophy on the other hand, the object is not present; what is more, philosophy has no object to begin with. It is a process which must at all times achieve being (in *its* appropriate manifestness) anew. Only in this process can philosophical truth disclose itself. For this reason it is crucial that

the listener should take the different steps in the process after
and with the lecturer.

What step have we taken? What step must we take over
and over again?

First we considered the following proposition as a fact:
The word "being" has a vague meaning; it is almost an empty
word. Closer discussion of this fact revealed: the vagueness of
this meaning finds its explanation: 1) in the blurring characteristic of the infinitive, 2) in the mixture into which all three
of the original stem meanings entered.

We designated the fact thus explained as the unshaken
point of departure of all the traditional metaphysical questioning about "being." It starts from the *essent* and is oriented
toward it. It does *not* start from being and does not enter into
the questionable nature of *its* manifestness. Because the meaning and concept of "being" have supreme universality, metaphysics as "physics" cannot go higher to define them more
closely. It has only one way left, from the universal to the
particular essent. In this way, it is true, it fills in the emptiness
of the concept of being, namely with the essents. Yet the admonition "Away from being; go to the particular essents,"
shows that metaphysics is mocking itself without knowing it.

For the much-vaunted particular essent can only disclose
itself as such insofar as we already understand being in *its*
essence.

Some light has been thrown on this essence. But it has not
yet been drawn into the area of questioning.

Now let us recall the question we asked in the beginning: Is
"being" only an empty word? Or are being and the asking of
the question of being the crux of the spiritual history of the
West?

Is being merely the last cloudy streak of evaporating reality;
is the only possible attitude for us to let it evaporate into complete indifference? Or is being the worthiest of all questions?

Thus inquiring, we take the decisive step from an indifferent fact, from the supposed meaninglessness of the word "being," to the supremely problematic phenomenon that being
necessarily discloses itself in our understanding.

The seemingly unshakable bald fact so blindly trusted by
metaphysics has been shaken.

Thus far in our inquiry about being we have striven primarily to grasp the word according to its form and meaning. Now it becomes clear that the question of being is not a matter of grammar and etymology. If in spite of this we again take language as our starting point, a special status must, here and in general, be accorded to the relation between being and language.

Ordinarily language, the word, is regarded as an expression of experience, which follows in the wake of experience. Insofar as things and occurrences are experienced in these experiences, language is indeed an expression, a copy as it were, of the experienced essent. The word "watch" for example, permits the well-known threefold differentiation; it may be considered: 1) in respect to the audible and visible form of the word; 2) in respect to the meaning of what we represent in connection with it; 3) in respect to the thing: a watch, this particular watch. Here 1) is a sign for 2) and 2) is an indication of 3).

Thus presumably we may do the same with the word "being," that is, differentiate word form, word meaning, and thing. And we easily see that as long as we dwell on the word form and its meaning we have not yet come to the "thing," to the point as it were of our question about being. If we expect to apprehend the essence of the thing, here of being, by mere discussions of the word and its meaning, we shall obviously be making a mistake. We are hardly likely to fall into such an error, for it would be like trying to investigate the phenomena of motion in the ether, in matter, to determine the atomic processes, by grammatical studies of the words "atom" and "ether" rather than by the necessary physical experiments.

Thus, regardless of whether the word "being" has an indefinite or a definite meaning, or, as we have seen, both at once, we must, beyond the factor of signification, come to the thing itself. But is "being" a thing like watches, houses, or any essent whatsoever? We have already run into the troublesome circumstance that being is not an essent and not an essent component of the essent. The being of the building over there is not just *another* thing of the *same* kind as the roof or the cellar. No thing corresponds to the word and the meaning "being."

But from this we cannot infer that being consists only of

the word and its meaning. The meaning of the word does not, as a meaning, constitute the essence of being. If it did, this would mean that the being of the essent, of our building for example, consisted in a word meaning. It would obviously be absurd to suppose any such thing. No; in the word "being," in its meaning, we pass through word and meaning and aim at being itself, except that it is not a thing, if by thing we mean something that is in any way essent.

From this it follows that in respect to the word "being" and its inflections, and all the words lying within its sphere, word and meaning are more profoundly dependent on what is meant than in the case of other words. But the converse is also true. Being itself is dependent on the word in a totally different and more fundamental sense than any essent.

In each of its inflections the word "being" bears an essentially different relation to being itself from that of all other nouns and verbs of the language to the essent that is expressed in them.

From this it may be inferred that the foregoing considerations regarding the word "being" are of greater import than other remarks about words and linguistic usage in connection with things of any sort whatsoever. But even though we have here a very special and fundamental connection between word, meaning, and being, in which so to speak the thing is missing, we must not suppose that it will be possible to sift out the essence of being itself from a characterization of the word meaning.

After regarding the peculiar phenomenon that the question of being remains intimately bound up with the question of the word, we resume the course of our questioning. We must show that our understanding of being has a determinateness of its own, ordained by being itself. Now when we start from discourse about being, because in a certain sense we are always and essentially compelled to take this as our starting point, we shall try to bear in mind the being itself of which the discourse speaks. We select a simple and familiar and almost careless kind of discourse where being is uttered in a word form whose use is so frequent that we scarcely notice it.

We say: "God is." "The earth is." "The lecture is in the auditorium." "This man is from Swabia." "The cup is of silver."

"The peasant is to the fields." "The book is mine." "Red is the port side." "There is famine in Russia." "The enemy is in retreat." "The plant louse is in the vineyard." "The dog is in the garden." "Über allen Gipfeln/ ist Ruh."*

In each case the "is" is meant differently. Of this we may easily convince ourselves, particularly if we take this utterance of the "is" as it really occurs, i.e. spoken in each case out of a definite situation, purpose, and mood, and not as a mere sentence or stale example in a grammar.

"God is"; i.e. he is *really present.* "The earth is"; i.e. we experience and believe it to be *permanently there;* "the lecture is in the auditorium"; i.e. it *takes place.* "The man is from Swabia"; i.e. *he comes from there.* "The cup is of silver"; i.e. it *is made of* . . . "The peasant is to the fields"; he has gone to the fields and is *staying there.* "The book is mine"; i.e. it *belongs to me.* "Red is the port side"; i.e. it *stands for* port. "The dog is in the garden"; i.e. he is *running around* in the garden. "Over all the summits/ is rest"; that is to say??? Does the "is" in these lines mean is situated, is present, takes places, abides? None of these will fit. And yet it is the same simple "is." Or does the verse mean: Over all the summits peace *prevails,* as quiet prevails in a classroom? No, that won't do either. Or perhaps: Over all the summits lies rest—or holds sway? That seems better, but it also misses the mark.

"Über allen Gipfeln/ ist Ruh"; the "ist" cannot be paraphrased and yet it is only this "ist," tossed off in those few lines that Goethe wrote in pencil on the window frame of a mountain hut near Ilmenau (cf. his letter to Zelter of September 4, 1831). Strange how we hesitate in our attempted paraphrase and in the end drop it altogether, not because the understanding is too complicated or difficult but because the line is spoken so simply, even more simply and uniquely than any of the other familiar "ises" that are forever dropping unnoticed into our everyday speech.

* I have omitted one of the examples from the translation: "Er ist des Todes," meaning literally "he is of death," or as Heidegger explains below, "er ist dem Tode verfallen," "he has succumbed to death."

"Der Bauer ist aufs Feld" ("The peasant is to the fields") is a popular expression in German, not poetic as it would be in English were anyone to use it. R.M.

Regardless of how we interpret these examples, they show one thing clearly: in the "is" being discloses itself to us in a diversity of ways. Once again the assertion, which at first seemed plausible, that being is an empty word is shown—more compellingly than ever—to be untrue.

But—it might here be argued—granted that the "is" is meant in many different ways. This springs not from the "is" itself but solely from the diverse content of the statements, each of which applies to a different essent: God, earth, cup, peasant, book, famine, peace over the summits. Only because the "is" remains intrinsically indeterminate and devoid of meaning can it lie ready for such diverse uses, can it fulfill and determine itself "as the circumstances require." The diversity of definite meanings cited above proves the contrary of what was to be shown. It offers the clearest proof that in order to be determinable being must be indeterminate.

What shall we say in reply to this? Here we come into the area of a decisive question: Does the "is" become manifold on the strength of the content brought to it in the different sentences, i.e. by virtue of the realms concerning which they speak, or does the "is," i.e. being, conceal within itself the multiplicity whose concentration ⟨Faltung, lit. "folding" in contrast to "unfolding"⟩ enables us to make manifold essents accessible to us, each *as* it is? For the present I merely throw out this question. We are not yet equipped to develop it further. What cannot be argued away—and this is the only point we wish to make for the moment—is that the "is" in our discourse manifests a rich diversity of meanings. In each one of these meanings we say the "is" without, either before or afterward, effecting a special exegesis of "is," let alone reflecting on being. The "is," meant now so and now so, simply wells up as we speak. Yet the diversity of its meanings is not arbitrary diversity. Let us now convince ourselves of this.

We run through the different meanings that we have interpreted by paraphrase. The "being" uttered in "is" means: really present, permanently there, takes place, come from, belongs to, is made of, stays, succumbs to, stands for, has entered upon, has appeared. It remains difficult, perhaps impossible, because contrary to the essence of being, to pick out a common meaning as a universal generic concept under which all these modes of "is" might be classified as species. Yet a single determinate trait runs through them all. It directs our contemplation of "being" to a definite horizon, in which understanding is effected. The limitation of the meaning of "being" remains within the sphere of actuality and presence, of permanence and duration, of abiding and occurrence.

All this points in the direction of what we encountered when we characterized the Greek experience and interpretation of being. If we retain the usual interpretation of being, the word "being" takes its meaning from the unity and determinateness of the horizon which guided our understanding. In short: we understand the verbal substantive "Sein" through the infinitive, which in turn is related to the "is" and its diversity that we have described. The definite and particular verb form "is," the *third person singular of the present indicative,* has here a pre-eminent rank. We understand "being" not in regard to the "thou art," "you are," "I am," or "they would be," though all of these, just as much as "is," represent verbal inflections of "to be." "To be" ⟨ sein ⟩ is for us the infinitive of "is." And involuntarily, almost as though nothing else were possible, we explain the infinitive "to be" to ourselves through the "is."

Accordingly, "being" has the meaning indicated above, recalling the Greek view of the essence of being, hence a determinateness which has not just dropped on us accidentally from somewhere but has dominated our historical being-there since antiquity. At one stroke our search for the definition of the meaning of the word "being" becomes explicitly what it is, namely a reflection on the source of our hidden history. The question "How does it stand with being?" must itself remain within the history of being if it is, in turn, to unfold and preserve its own historical import. In pursuing it we, in turn, shall hold to the discourse of being.

4.

THE LIMITATION OF BEING

Just as in the "is" we have a thoroughly familiar mode of discourse of being, so in the noun "being" we run into very definite modes of discourse that have even taken on a quality of formulas: being and becoming; being and appearance; being and thinking; being and the ought.

When we say "being" we tend, almost as though under compulsion, to continue: being and . . . This "and" does not mean only that we casually throw in something else; no, we are adding something from which "being" is distinguished: being *and not* . . . But in these formula-like titles we also mean something which, differentiated from being, somehow belongs intrinsically to being, if only as its Other.

The course of our questioning up to this point has illuminated more than its range. True, for the present we have perceived the question itself, the fundamental question of metaphysics, as a question proposed to us from somewhere outside. But we have come appreciably closer to an understanding of the value of this question. More and more it has proved to be a hidden ground of our historical being-there. This it remains even, and particularly, when, self-satisfied and busy with all manner of things, we move about over this ground as over a flimsily covered abyss ⟨ Ab-grund ⟩.

Now we shall pursue the distinctions between being and other concepts. In so doing we shall learn that, contrary to the opinion current in this country, being is anything but an empty word and is indeed determined in so many aspects that we have difficulty in orienting ourselves so as to keep a sufficient grip on the determinateness. But this is not enough. The experience must be developed into a fundamental experience of our future historical being-there. In order that we may from the very outset effect (and participate in) the distinctions in the proper way, it may be well to give the following pointers:

1. Being is delimited from something else; in this delimitation it already has determinateness.

2. It is delimited in four interrelated respects. Accordingly, the determinateness of being must either become ramified and heightened or else diminish.

3. These distinctions are by no means accidental. What is held apart in them belonged originally together and tends to merge. The distinctions therefore have an inner necessity.

4. Consequently the oppositions, which look at first sight like formulas, did not arise fortuitously and find their way into the language as figures of speech. They arose in close connection with the development of the concept of being, a process crucial for the history of the West. They began with the beginning of philosophical questioning.

5. These distinctions have remained dominant not only in Western philosophy. They permeate all knowledge, action, and discourse even where they are not specifically mentioned or not in these words.

6. The order in which the titles have been listed provides in itself an indication of the order in which they are internally linked and of the historical order in which they were shaped.

The first two distinctions (being and becoming, being and appearance) were developed at the very beginning of Greek philosophy. As the oldest, they are also the best known.

The third distinction (being and thinking) was foreshadowed as early as the first two; its decisive unfolding occurred in the philosophy of Plato and Aristotle, but it took on its actual form only with the beginning of the modern era. It even played an essential part in this beginning. As its history suggests, it is the most complex of the four distinctions and the most problematic in purpose. (For this reason it remains for us the one most worthy of questioning.)

The fourth distinction (being and the ought) was only remotely foreshadowed by the designation of the *on* ⟨ the essent, that which is ⟩ as *agathon* ⟨ the good ⟩. It belongs wholly to the modern era. And since the end of the eighteenth century it has determined one of the dominant positions of the modern spirit toward the essent in general.

7. If one is to ask the question of being radically, one must understand the task of unfolding the truth of the essence of being; one must come to a decision regarding the powers hidden in these distinctions in order to restore them to their own truth.

All these preliminary remarks should be borne constantly in mind in connection with the following considerations.

1. Being and Becoming

This distinction and opposition stands at the beginning of the inquiry into being. Today it is still the most current restriction of being by something other; for it comes directly to mind from the standpoint of a conception of being that has congealed into the self-evident. What becomes is not yet. What is need no longer become. What "is," the essent, has left all becoming behind it if indeed it ever became or could become. What "is" in the authentic sense also resists every onsurge of becoming.

Parmenides lived at the turn of the fifth century B.C. Farsighted thinker and poet, he set forth the being of the essent in contradistinction to becoming. His "didactic poem" has come down to us only in fragments, but in large and important ones. Here I shall cite only a few verses (Fragment 8, lines 1–6):

But only the legend remains of the way
(along which it is disclosed) how it stands with being; on this
    (way) there are many indications:
  how being, without genesis, is without destruction,
  complete ⟨ voll-ständig, fully standing ⟩, alone there
  without tremor and not still requiring to be finished;
  nor was it before, nor will it be in the future,

> for being present it *is* entirely, unique, unifying, united,
> gathering itself in itself from itself (cohesive,
> full of presentness).*

These few words stand there like the Greek statues of the early period. What we still possess of Parmenides' didactic poem fits into a thin brochure, but this little brochure is one which might perfectly well replace whole libraries of supposedly indispensable philosophical literature. Anyone living today who knows the measure of such thinking discourse must lose all desire to write books.

What is said here from within the heart of being consists of *sēmata*, not signs of being, not predicates, but indications which in looking-toward being from within being indicate being. For in thus looking-toward being we must, in an active sense, look-away from all coming-into-being and passing-away, etc.: in the act of seeing we must hold them away, expel them. What is kept away by *a-* and *oude* is not commensurate with being. It has another measure.

To this discourse, we conclude, being appears as the pure fullness of the permanent, gathered within it, untouched by unrest and change. Even today it is customary in describing the beginning of Western philosophy to oppose the doctrine of Heraclitus to this doctrine of Parmenides. A much-quoted saying is attributed to Heraclitus: *panta rhei*, everything is in flux. Accordingly there is no being. Everything "is" becoming.

The occurrence of such oppositions, here being, there becoming, is accepted as perfectly natural, because it seems to provide an example, from the very beginning of philosophy, of a state of affairs that is supposed to run through the whole history of philosophy, namely that where one philosopher says A, another will say B, but that if the second says A, the first will say B. Yet when it is argued in answer to this supposition that all thinkers throughout the history of philosophy have said fundamentally the same thing, this too seems to

---

* μόνος δ' ἔτι μῦθος ὁδοῖο/ λείπεται ὡς ἔστιν. ταύτηι δ' ἐπὶ σήματ' ἔασι/ πολλὰ μάλ', ὡς ἀγένητον ἐὸν ἀνώλεθρόν ἐστιν, ἔστι γὰρ οὐλομελές τε καὶ ἀτρεμὲς ἠδ' ἀτέλεστον, οὐδέ ποτ' ἦν οὐδ' ἔσται, ἐπεὶ νῦν ἔστιν ὁμοῦ πᾶν,/ ἕν, συνεχές.

impose on common sense. If they all say the same thing, why the whole multifarious and complicated history of Western philosophy? If that were so, *one* philosophy would suffice. And yet this "sameness" has an inner truth, namely the inexhaustible richness of what on every single day is as though that day were its first.

Actually Heraclitus, to whom is ascribed the doctrine of becoming as diametrically opposed to Parmenides' doctrine of being, says the same as Parmenides. He would not be one of the greatest of the great Greeks if he had said something different. But his doctrine of becoming must not be interpreted in line with the ideas of nineteenth-century Darwinism. It is true that the opposition between being and becoming was never again represented so uniquely and self-sufficiently as in Parmenides. In that great age, in Parmenides, the saga of the being of the essent itself partakes of the (hidden) essence of the being of which it speaks. The secret of greatness resides in its historic necessity. For reasons that will become clear in the following, we shall limit our present discussion of this first distinction—"being and becoming"—to these few indications.

2. Being and Appearance

This distinction is as old as the first. The fact that the two distinctions (being and becoming, being and appearance) are equally primordial points to a profound connection between them. Hitherto this connection has been inaccessible to us. It has not been possible to redevelop the second distinction (being and appearance) in its true meaning. To do so one must understand it in its original, i.e. Greek, sense. For us, burdened as we are with the modern epistemological misinterpretation —for us who scarcely respond, and then for the most part emptily, to the simplicity of the essential—this is no easy matter.

At first sight the distinction seems clear. Being and appearance means: the real in contradistinction to the unreal; the authentic over against the inauthentic. The distinction implies an evaluation—the preference is given to being. As we say: the miracle and the miraculous, so we say appearance and the apparent. Often the distinction between being and appearance is carried back to our first distinction—being and becoming. The apparent is that which from time to time emerges and vanishes, the ephemeral and unstable over against being as the permanent.

The distinction between being and appearance is familiar to us, another of the many worn-out coins that we pass unexamined from hand to hand in an everyday life that has grown flat. When it turns up, we use the distinction as a rule of life, a moral admonition to avoid appearance and to strive for being: "to be rather than seem."

Yet familiar and self-evident as the distinction is, we do not understand in what way a fundamental separation occurs between precisely being and appearance. The very fact that it occurs suggests that the two are related. Wherein does the bond consist? First we must understand the hidden unity of being and appearance. We have ceased to understand it because we have fallen away from the initial, historically developed difference and merely carry it around as something that was once, somewhere and at some time, put into circulation.

To grasp the difference we must here again go back to the beginning.

But if, before it is too late, we turn our backs on idle, thoughtless chatter, we shall find, even in ourselves, a track leading to the understanding of the difference. We say "appearance" and we know the rain and the sunshine. The sun shines ⟨ scheinen, "to seem" and "to shine" ⟩. We say: "the room was feebly lighted by the glow ⟨ Schein ⟩ of a candle." The Alemanic dialect has the word "Scheinholz," wood that glows in the darkness. From pictures of saints we know the halo ⟨ Heiligenschein ⟩, the glowing ring about their heads. But we also know pseudo saints ⟨ Scheinheilige ⟩, those who look like saints but are not saints. We are familiar with the sham battle ⟨ Scheingefecht ⟩ or simulated battle. The sun, as it shines ⟨ scheint ⟩ seems ⟨ scheint ⟩ to move around the earth. The moon which shines seems, but only seems, to measure two feet in diameter, that is only an illusion ⟨ Schein ⟩. Here we run into two different kinds of Schein and scheinen. But they do not simply stand side by side; no, one is a variant of the other. The sun, for example, can have the appearance ⟨Schein⟩ of moving round the earth only because it shines, i.e. glows and in glowing manifests itself, i.e. comes to light ⟨zum Vor*schein*⟩. In the shining of the sun, to be sure, we at the same time experience its radiation as heat. The sun shines: it shows itself and we feel warmth. In the halo the shining of the light makes the wearer manifest ⟨bringt zum Vorschein⟩ as a saint.

On closer scrutiny we find three modes of Schein: 1) Schein as radiance and glow; 2) Schein and Scheinen as appearing, as coming to light; 3) Schein as mere appearance or semblance ⟨Anschein⟩. But at the same time it becomes clear that the second variety of "Scheinen," appearing in the sense of showing itself, pertains both to Schein as radiance and to Schein as semblance, and not as a fortuitous attribute but as the ground of their possibility. The essence of appearance ⟨Schein⟩ lies in the appearing ⟨Erscheinen⟩. It is self-manifestation, self-representation, standing-there, presence. The long-awaited book has just appeared, i.e. it is before us, and therefore to be had. When we say: the moon shines ⟨scheint⟩, this means not only that it spreads a glow ⟨Schein⟩, a certain brightness, but also: it stands in the sky, it is present, it is. The stars shine: glittering, they are present. Here appearance ⟨Schein⟩ means exactly the same as being. (Sappho's verses: *asteres men amphi kalan sellanan* . . . and the poem by Matthias Claudius, "Ein Wiegenlied bei Mondschein zu singen," provide a suitable basis for reflection on being and appearance.)

If we meditate on the above, we find the inner connection between being and appearance. But we grasp it fully only if we understand being in an equally primordial, i.e. Greek, sense. We know that being disclosed itself to the Greeks as *physis*. The realm of emerging and abiding is intrinsically at the same time a shining appearing ⟨das scheinende Erscheinen⟩. The radicals *phy* and *pha* name the same thing. *Phyein*, self-sufficient emergence, is *phainesthai*, to flare up, to show itself, to appear. Already the traits of being that we have meanwhile listed without really going into them, and our reference to Parmenides, have given us a certain understanding of the basic Greek word for being.

It would be instructive to elucidate the meaning of this word through the great poetry of the Greeks. Here it may suffice to point out that for Pindar *phya* was the fundamental determination of man's being-there: *to de phya krattiston*, that which is through and from out of *phya* is the mightiest of all (Olympian Ode IX, 100); *phya* means what one originally and authentically is: the past and essential ⟨ das Ge-Wesende ⟩ as opposed to the subsequently imposed bustle and pretense. Being is the fundamental attribute of the noble individual and of nobility (i.e. of what has a high origin and rests in it). In regard to this Pindar coins the saying *genoi' hoios essi mathōn* (Pythian Ode II, 72). "Mayest thou by learning come forth as what thou art." But for the Greeks standing-in-itself was nothing other than standing-there, standing-in-the-light. Being means appearing. Appearing is not something subsequent that sometimes happens to being. Appearing is the very essence of being.

This punctures the empty construction of Greek philosophy as a "realistic" philosophy which, unlike modern subjectivism, was a doctrine of objective being. This widespread conception is based on a superficial understanding. We must leave aside terms like "subjective" and "objective," "realistic" and "idealistic."

Only now are we in a position, on the basis of a more appropriate view of being as the Greeks saw it, to take the decisive step which will open up to us the inner relationship between being and appearance; to gain an insight into a relationship which is originally and uniquely Greek but which compassed characteristic consequences for the spirit of the West. The essence of being is *physis*. Appearing is the power that emerges. Appearing makes manifest. Already we know then that being, appearing, causes to emerge from concealment. Since the essent as such *is*, it places itself in and stands in *unconcealment, alētheia*. We translate, and at the same time thoughtlessly misinterpret, this word as "truth." To be sure, people are gradually beginning to translate the Greek word *alētheia* literally. But this does not help much if one goes right on to construe "truth" in a totally different un-Greek sense and attribute this other sense to the Greek word. For the Greek essence of truth is possible only in one with the

Greek essence of being as *physis*. On the strength of the unique and essential relationship between *physis* and *alētheia* the Greeks would have said: The essent is true insofar as it is. The true as such is essent. This means: The power that manifests itself stands in unconcealment. In showing itself, the unconcealed as such comes to stand. Truth as un-concealment is not an appendage to being.

Truth is inherent in the essence of being. To be an essent —this comprises to come to light, to appear on the scene, to take one's ⟨its⟩ place ⟨sich hin-stellen⟩, to produce ⟨her-stellen⟩ something. Nonbeing, on the other hand, means: to withdraw from appearing, from presence. The essence of appearing includes coming-on-the-scene and withdrawing, hither and thither in the truly demonstrative, indicative sense. Being is thus dispersed among the manifold essents. These display themselves as the momentary and close-at-hand. In appearing it gives itself an aspect, *dokei*. *Doxa* means aspect, regard ⟨Ansehen⟩, namely the regard in which one stands. If the regard, in keeping with what emerges in it, is a distinguished one, *doxa* means fame and glory. In Hellenistic theology and in the New Testament *doxa theou*, gloria Dei, is God's grandeur. To glorify, to attribute regard to, and disclose regard means in Greek: to place in the light and thus endow with permanence, being. For the Greeks glory was not something additional which one might or might not obtain; it was the mode of the highest being. For moderns glory has long been nothing more than celebrity and as such a highly dubious affair, an acquisition tossed about and distributed by the newspapers and the radio—almost the opposite of being. If for Pindar to glorify was the essence of poetry and the work of the poet was to place in the light, it was not because the notion of light played a special role for him but solely because he thought and composed poetry as a Greek, which is to say that he stood in the appointed essence of being.

We wished to show that for the Greeks appearing belonged to being, or more precisely that the essence of being lay *partly* in appearing. This has been clarified through the supreme possibility of human being, as fashioned by the Greeks, through glory and glorification. Glory is in Greek *doxa*. *Dokeō* means:

I show myself, appear, enter into the light. Here the emphasis
is on sight and aspect, the regard in which a man stands; in
the other Greek word for glory, *kleos*, it is on hearing and calling. Thus glory is the fame ⟨ Ruf, call, reputation, fame ⟩ in
which one stands. Heraclitus says (Fragment 29): "for the
noblest choose one thing before all else: glory, everlastingly
abiding over against things mortal; but the many are glutted
like cattle."*

But to all this there comes a limitation which at the same
time indicates the full richness of the context. *Doxa* is the regard in which a man stands, in a broader sense the regard
⟨ Ansehen, looking-at, esteem ⟩ which every essent conceals
and discloses in its appearance ⟨ Aussehen ⟩ (*eidos, idea*). A
city presents a magnificent view. The aspect which an essent
has in itself, and which it can offer only for this reason, may
in every case be perceived from this or that point of view. According to the diversity of viewpoint, the aspect that offers
itself changes. Hence the aspect is always one that *we* take
and make for ourselves. In experiencing and dealing with essents, we are always forming views of their appearance. Often
we do so without looking closely at the thing itself. In various
ways and for various reasons we form a view of the thing. We
form an opinion about it. Sometimes the view that we advocate has no support in the thing itself. Then it is only a view,
an assumption. We assume a thing to be thus or thus. Then all
we have is an opinion. To assume is in Greek *dechesthai*. (Acceptance remains related to the offer of the appearance.)
Doxa as something assumed to be thus and thus is opinion.

Now we have come to the point at which we were aiming.
Because being, *physis*, consists in appearing, in an offering of
appearance and views, it stands, essentially and hence necessarily and permanently, in the possibility of an appearance
which precisely covers over and conceals what the essent in
truth, i.e. in unconcealment, is. This regard in which the essent now comes to stand is *Schein* in the sense of Anschein
⟨ semblance ⟩. Where there is unconcealment of the essent,
there is a possibility of Schein and conversely: where the es-

---

* αἱρεῦνται γὰρ ἓν ἀντὶ ἁπάντων οἱ ἄριστοι, κλέος ἀέναον
θνητῶν, οἱ δὲ πολλοὶ κεκόρηνται ὅκωσπερ κτήνεα.

sent stands and has stood unwaveringly in Schein, the appearance ⟨ Schein ⟩ can shatter and fall away.

The word *doxa* is a name for diverse things: 1) regard as glory; 2) regard as sheer vision that offers something; 3) regard as mere looking-so: "appearance" as mere semblance; 4) view that a man forms, opinion. The many meanings of this word are not the result of careless speech; they are a playing deeply grounded in the mature wisdom of a great language which in this word preserves essential traits of being. For a sound approach to this matter we must take care not to falsify appearance by taking it as something merely "imagined," "subjective." No, appearance, just as much as appearing, belongs to the essent.

Let us think of the sun. Every day it rises and sets for us. Only a very few astronomers, physicists, philosophers—and even they only on the basis of a specialized approach which may be more or less widespread—experience this state of affairs otherwise, namely as a motion of the earth around the sun. But the appearance in which sun and earth stand, e.g. the early morning landscape, the sea in the evening, the night, is an appearing. This appearance is not nothing. Nor is it untrue. Nor is it a mere appearance of conditions in nature which are really otherwise. This appearance is historical and it is history, discovered and grounded in poetry and myth and thus an essential area of our world.

Only the tired latecomers with their supercilious wit imagine that they can dispose of the historical power of appearance by declaring it to be "subjective," hence very dubious. The Greeks experienced it differently. They were perpetually compelled to wrest being from appearance and preserve it against appearance. (The essence of being is un-concealment.)

Solely in the enduring struggle between being and appearance did they wrest being from the essent, did they carry the essent to permanence and unconcealment: the gods and the state, the temples and the tragedy, the games and philosophy; all this in the midst of appearance, beset by appearance, but also taking it seriously, knowing of its power. It was in the Sophists and in Plato that appearance was declared to be mere appearance and thus degraded. At the same time being, as *idea*, was exalted to a suprasensory realm. A chasm, *chōrismos,*

was created between the merely apparent essent here below
and real being somewhere on high. In that chasm Christianity
settled down, at the same time reinterpreting the lower as the
created and the higher as the creator. These refashioned weap-
ons it turned against antiquity (as paganism) and so disfig-
ured it. Nietzsche was right in saying that Christianity is Plato-
nism for the people.

Distinct from all this, the great age of Greece was a single
creative self-assertion amid the confused, intricate struggle
between the powers of being and appearance. (In regard to
the original relation between human being-there, being as
such, and truth in the sense of unconcealment and untruth
as concealment, see *Sein und Zeit* §§ 44 and 68.)

For the thinking of the early Greek thinkers the unity and
conflict of being and appearance preserved their original
power. All this was represented with supreme purity in Greek
tragic poetry. Let us consider the *Oedipus Rex* of Sophocles.
At the beginning Oedipus is the savior and lord of the state,
living in an aura of glory and divine favor. He is hurled out of
this appearance, which is not merely his subjective view of
himself but the medium in which his being-there appears; his
being as murderer of his father and desecrator of his mother
is raised to unconcealment. The way from the radiant beginning to the gruesome end is one struggle between appearance
(concealment and distortion) and unconcealment (being).
The city is beset by the secret of the murderer of Laius, the
former king. With the passion of a man who stands in the
manifestness of glory and is a Greek, Oedipus sets out to reveal this secret. Step by step, he must move into unconcealment, which in the end he can bear only by putting out his
own eyes, i.e. by removing himself from all light, by letting
the cloak of night fall round him, and, blind, crying out to
the people to open all doors in order that a man may be
made manifest to them as what he *is*.

But we cannot regard Oedipus only as the man who meets
his downfall; we must see him as the embodiment of Greek
being-there, who most radically and wildly asserts its fundamental passion, the passion for disclosure of being, i.e. the
struggle for being itself. In his poem "In lieblicher Bläue
blühet . . ." Hölderlin wrote keen-sightedly: "Perhaps King

Oedipus has an eye too many." This eye too many is the fundamental condition for all great questioning and knowledge and
also their only metaphysical ground. The knowledge and the
science of the Greeks were this passion.

Today science is admonished to serve the nation, and that
is a very necessary and estimable demand, but it is too little
and not the essential. The hidden will to refashion the essent
into the manifestness of its being demands more. In order to
recapture the pristine knowledge that has degenerated into
science, our being-there must attain a very different metaphysical depth. It must once again achieve an established and
truly built relation to the being of the essent as a whole.

Our relation to everything that makes up being, truth, and
appearance has long been so confused, so devoid of foundation and passion, that even in our manner of interpreting Greek
poetry and making it our own we barely suspect the power
wielded by this poetic discourse in Greek being-there. Karl
Reinhardt's recent interpretation of Sophocles (1933) comes
appreciably closer to Greek being-there and being than all
previous attempts, because Reinhardt sees and questions the
tragic process on the basis of the fundamental relations between being, unconcealment, and appearance. Though modern subjectivisms and psychologisms still find their way into
it, his interpretation of the *Oedipus Rex* as the "tragedy of appearance" remains a magnificent achievement.

I shall conclude this reference to the poetic form of the
struggle between being and appearance among the Greeks
by quoting a passage from Sophocles' *Oedipus Rex*, which will
permit us, without forcing matters, to establish the connection
between our provisional characterization of Greek being as
stability and the characterization, now attained, of being as
appearing.

The brief final chorus of the tragedy (lines 1189 ff.) runs:
"What man has in him more controlled and ordered being-
there than he requires to stand in appearance and then, having done so, to incline (namely from standing-straight-in-
himself)?"*

---

* τίς γὰρ τίς ἀνὴρ πλέον
  τᾶς εὐδαιμονίας φέρει
  ἢ τοσοῦτον ὅσον δοκεῖν
  καὶ δόξαντ' ἀποκλῖναι.

In explaining the essence of the infinitive, we spoke of certain words that represent an *enklisis,* a bending-away, a falling-over (*casus*). Now we see that appearance as a variant of being is the same as a falling-over. It is a variant of being in the sense of standing-there-upright-in-oneself. Both deviations from being are determined on the basis of being as permanent standing-in-the-light, i.e. appearing.

Now it has become clearer that appearance belongs to being itself as appearing. Being as appearance is no less a power than being as unconcealment. Appearance takes place in and with the essent itself. But appearance not only makes the essent as such appear as what it actually is not; it not only distorts the essent whose appearance it is; no, it even cloaks itself as appearance insofar as it shows itself as being. Because appearance thus essentially distorts itself in its cloaking and dissembling, we rightly say that appearance deceives. This deception lies in the appearance itself. Only because appearance itself deceives can it deceive man and lead him into illusion. But illusion is only one among the modes according to which man moves in the interlocking threefold world of being, unconcealment, and appearance.

The area, as it were, which opens in the interwovenness of being, unconcealment, and appearance—this area I understand as *error.* Appearance, deception, illusion, error stand in definite essential and dynamic relations which have long been misinterpreted by psychology and epistemology and which consequently, in our daily lives, we have well-nigh ceased to experience and recognize as powers.

It has been necessary to show how, on the basis of the Greek interpretation of being as *physis, and only on* this basis, both *truth* in the sense of unconcealment and *appearance* as a definite mode of emerging self-manifestation belong necessarily to being.

Because being and appearance belong together and, belonging together, are always side by side, the one changing unceasingly into the other; because in this change they present the possibility of error and confusion, the main effort of thought at the beginning of philosophy, i.e. in the first disclosure of the being of the essent, was necessarily to rescue being from its plight of being submerged in appearance, to

differentiate being from appearance. This in turn made it
necessary to secure the priority of truth as unconcealment
over concealment, of discovery over occultation and distortion. But as it became necessary to differentiate being from
the other and to consolidate it as *physis*, being was differentiated from nonbeing, while nonbeing was differentiated from
appearance. The two differentiations do not coincide.

Because of this relation between being, unconcealment, appearance, and nonbeing, the man who holds to being as it
opens round him and whose attitude toward the essent is determined by his adherence to being, must take three paths.
If he is to take over being-there in the radiance of being, he
must bring being to stand, he must endure it in appearance
and against appearance, and he must wrest both appearance
and being from the abyss of nonbeing.

Man must distinguish these three ways and accordingly
he must decide for them and against them. Thought at the
beginning of philosophy was the opening and laying-out of
the three paths. Discrimination ⟨ das Unterscheiden ⟩ placed
sapient man on these paths and at their crossing, hence in a
permanent decision ⟨ Ent-scheidung ⟩. It is with this decision
that history begins. Even the decision concerning the gods
resided in this decision and in it alone. (Accordingly decision
means here not man's judgment and choice, but a separation
in the above-mentioned togetherness of being, unconcealment,
appearance, and nonbeing.)

The philosophy of Parmenides, as it has come down to us
in his didactic poem, is our oldest record of the opening of
these three paths. We may characterize the three paths by
quoting a few fragments of the poem. A complete commentary is not possible here.

In translation, Fragment 4 runs:

> Come, I will tell you: heed well the words that you
> hear (as to) which ways of inquiry are alone to be considered.
> The one: how it is (how it, being, is), and how also nonbeing
>   (is) impossible.
> This is the path of justified confidence, for it follows uncon-
>   cealment.
> The other: that it is not and also that nonbeing (is) necessary.

This then, I tell you, is a path which cannot be counseled,
neither can you make acquaintance with nonbeing, for it can-
      not be brought forward,
nor can you indicate it in words.

Here, for the present, two paths are sharply marked off
from one another:

1. The path to being; it is at the same time the way to unconcealment. This path is inevitable.

2. The path to nonbeing; to be sure, it cannot be traveled,
but for this very reason it must be made known that this path
is unviable, particularly in view of the fact that it leads to
nonbeing. This fragment provides perhaps the oldest philosophical statement to the effect that along with the way of
being the way of nonbeing must be specially *considered*,
that it is therefore a misunderstanding of the question of
being to turn one's back on nothing with the assurance that
nothing is obviously not. (For that nothing is not an essent
does not prevent it from belonging to being in its own way.)

But reflection on these two paths encompasses a coming-
to-grips with a third which runs counter to the first in a particular way. The third path looks like the first, but it does
not lead to being. It seems therefore to be no more than another way to nonbeing in the sense of nothing.

Fragment 6 starts by sharply opposing the two paths indicated in Fragment 4, the path to being and the path to
nothing. But then a third path is indicated, counter to the
second which leads to nothing and is therefore without issue.

Needful is the gathering setting-forth as well the apprehen-
      sion: the essent in its being;
For the essent has being; nonbeing has no "is"; this I bid you
      consider.
Above all avoid this way of questioning.
But also that other which men, knowing nothing, two-headed,
Cut out for themselves; for disorientation
Is the guide to their erring understanding; they are thrown
      hither and thither,
dull-witted, blind, perplexed; the brotherhood of those who
      do not differentiate,
whose dictum it is that the essent and nonessent are the same

and also not the same—to them in all ways the path is contrary.

The path now mentioned is that of *doxa* in the sense of appearance. Along this path the essent looks now thus and now otherwise. Here only opinions prevail. Men slide back and forth from one opinion to another. They mix being and appearance.

This path is perpetually traveled and on it men lose themselves entirely.

It is all the more necessary to know this path *as such*, in order that being may disclose itself in appearance and against appearance.

Accordingly we find this third path and its relation to the first indicated in Fragment 1, lines 28–32:

> . . . It is necessary (for you who are now entering on the path to being) to experience everything,
> the untrembling heart of well-rounded unconcealment as well as the views of men, in which there dwells no reliance on the unconcealed.
> But with all this you should also learn how appearance persists in appearingly drawing (in its own way) through all things, contributing to complete all things.

The third path is that of appearance, but in a particular way, for on this path appearance is experienced *as* belonging to being. For the Greeks the words we have quoted possessed an original force. Being and truth draw their essence from *physis*. The self-manifestation of the apparent belongs immediately to being and yet again (fundamentally) does not belong to it. Therefore appearing must be exposed as mere appearance, and this over and over again.

Intrinsically the indications of the threefold path are one:
The path to being is inevitable.
The path to nothing is inaccessible.
The path to appearance is always accessible and traveled, but one can go around it.

A truly sapient man is therefore not one who blindly pursues a truth, but only one who is always cognizant of all three paths, that of being, that of nonbeing, and that of appearance. Superior knowledge—and all knowledge is superiority—is given only to the man who has known the buoyant storm on the path of being, who has known the dread of the second path to the abyss of nothing, but who has taken upon himself the third way, the arduous path of appearance.

This knowledge includes what the Greeks in their great age called *tolma:* to undertake the venture of being, nonbeing, and appearance all at once, i.e. to take upon oneself being-there as a de-cision between being, nonbeing, and appearance. From out of this fundamental attitude toward being, one of their greatest poets, Pindar (Nemean Ode III, 70), said: *en de peirai telos diaphainetai;* in venturesome exploration of the essent is manifested perfection, the limitation of that which has been brought, and come, to stand, i.e. being.

Here speaks the same basic attitude that shines forth from Heraclitus' saying about *polemos.* It is struggle, setting-apart ⟨Aus-einander-Setzung⟩, i.e. not mere quarreling and wrangling but the conflict of the conflicting, that sets the essential and the nonessential, the high and the low, in their limits and makes them manifest.

The mature certainty of this attitude toward being is as boundlessly admirable as the richness of its configurations in words and in stone.

We conclude our elucidation of the opposition, i.e. at the same time, the unity, of being and appearance with a saying of Heraclitus (Fragment 123): *physis kryptesthai philei.* "Being (emerging appearing) inclines intrinsically to self-concealment." Since being means emerging appearing, to issue forth from concealment—concealment, its origin in concealment, belongs to it essentially. This origin lies in the essence of being, of the manifest as such. Being inclines back toward it, both in great silence and mystery and in banal distortion and occultation. The close relation between *physis* and *kryptesthai* discloses both the intimate bond and the conflict between being and appearance.

If we take the formula "being and appearance" in the undiminished force of the differentiation which the Greeks won at the beginning of their thinking, the difference and delimitation of being over against appearance become comprehensible, and moreover we understand its intimate relation with the differentiation between "being and becoming." What is situated in becoming is no longer nothing and it is not yet that which it is destined to become. In view of this "no longer and not yet," becoming is shot through with nonbeing. Yet it is not pure nothing, but no longer this and not yet that and as such perpetually other. Consequently it looks now this way and now that. It presents an intrinsically unstable aspect. Thus seen, becoming is an appearance of being.

In the initial disclosure of the being of the essent, it was therefore necessary to oppose becoming as well as appearance to being. On the other hand, becoming as "emerging" belongs to *physis*. If we take them both in the Greek sense— becoming as coming-into-presence and going-out of it; being as emerging, appearing presence; nonbeing as absence—then the reciprocal relation between emerging and declining is appearing, being itself. Just as becoming is the appearance of being, so appearance as appearing is a becoming of being.

This makes it clear that we may not simply reduce the distinction between "being and appearance" to that between "being and becoming," or the other way around. Consequently the question of the relation between the two distinctions will have to remain open for the present. The answer will depend on the radicalness, breadth, and solidity with which we ground the being of the essent. And in the beginning philosophy did not tie itself down to single propositions. The subsequent accounts of its history create the contrary impression, to be sure, for they are doxographical, i.e. a description of the opinions and views of the great thinkers. But anyone who searches the great thinkers for their opinions and viewpoints can be sure of going astray before obtaining a result, i.e. the formula or signpost for a philosophy. The *thinking* and being-there of the Greeks were a struggle for a decision between the great powers of being and becoming, being and appearance. Inevitably this struggle molded the relation between thinking and being into a definite form. The third distinction was beginning to take shape.

3. Being and Thinking

The crucial importance of the distinction between "being" and "thinking" in Western existence has often been pointed out. This pre-eminence must have its ground in the essence of the distinction, that is, in what sets it off from the first two and from the fourth as well. Hence I should like to begin by indicating its special character. First we shall compare it with those already discussed. In them what is distinguished from being comes to us from the essent itself. We find it in the realm of the essent. Not only becoming but also appearance confront us in the essent as such (cf. the rising and setting sun, the famous stick that looks broken when immersed in water, and so on). Becoming and appearance are situated as it were on the same plane as the being of the essent.

But in the distinction between *being and thinking*, not only is what is contrasted with being, namely thinking, different in content from becoming and appearance, but moreover the sense of the opposition is essentially different. Thinking sets itself off against being in such a way that being is placed before ⟨ vor-gestellt, represented ⟩ it and consequently stands opposed to it ⟨ entgegensteht ⟩ as an object ⟨ Gegenstand ⟩. This is not the case in the previous distinctions. Now we see how this distinction can achieve a pre-eminence. It predominates because it does not situate itself in between and among the other three decisions but represents them all, and thus representing them ⟨ vorsichstellend, placing them before itself ⟩ transposes ⟨ umstellt ⟩ them, as it were. So it comes about that thinking is not merely the contrary member of some new distinction but the foundation and fulcrum on the basis of which the opposite is determined, so much so that being takes on its entire interpretation from thinking.

It is in this direction that we must appraise the significance of this differentiation for our present task. For fundamentally we are asking how it stands with being, how and whence its essence is established, understood, grasped, and posited as the determining category.

In the seemingly unimportant distinction between being

and thinking we must discern the fundamental position of the Western spirit, against which our central attack is directed. It can be overcome only by a return to its *origins*, i.e. we must place its initial truth within its own limits and so put it on a new foundation.

From the vantage point to which our questioning has now brought us we can survey another aspect. We have shown that, contrary to the current opinion, the word "being" has a strictly circumscribed meaning. This implies that being itself is understood in a definite way. Thus understood, it is manifest to us. But all understanding, as a fundamental mode of disclosure, must move in a definite line of sight. The nature of this thing, the clock for example, remains closed to us unless we know something in advance about such things as time, reckoning with time, the measurement of time. The line of sight must be laid down in advance. We call it the "perspective," the track of fore-sight ⟨ Vorblickbahn ⟩. Thus we shall see not only that being is not understood in an indeterminate way but that the determinate understanding of being moves in a predetermined perspective.

To move back and forth, to slip and slide along this track have become second nature with us, so much so that we neither have knowledge of it nor even consider or understand the inquiry into it. We have become immersed (not to say lost) in this perspective, this line of sight which sustains and guides all our understanding of being. And what makes our immersion the more complete as well as the more hidden is that even the Greeks did not and could not bring this perspective to light, and this for essential reasons (not for reasons of human deficiency). Still, the growth of the differentiation between being and thinking played an important part in forming and stabilizing this perspective in which the Greek understanding of being moved.

Nevertheless we have accorded this distinction third and not first place. We shall first attempt to elucidate it in the same way as the first two.

We begin again with a general characterization of what is now opposed to being.

What does thinking mean? We say "Man thinks, God governs" ⟨ "der Mensch denkt, Gott lenkt," usually translated as

"man proposes, God disposes" ⟩. Here thinking means to con-
trive, to plan this and that; to think of something ⟨ denken
auf ⟩ means to have it in view, to aim at it. "To think evil"
means to intend evil; to think of ⟨ denken an ⟩ something means
not to forget it. Here thinking means to remember. We use the
turn of phrase "to think nothing of it." Here thinking means
to imagine. Someone says: I think it will turn out all right, i.e.
it seems to me; I am of the opinion. To think in an emphatic
sense means to reflect, to think something over, a situation, a
plan, an event. "Thinking" serves also as a name for the work
of those whom we call "thinkers." In contrast to animals, all
men think, but not every man is a thinker.

What do we infer from this linguistic usage? Thinking refers to the future as well as the past, but also to the present.
Thinking brings something before us, *represents it*. This representation always starts from ourselves, it is a free act, but
not an arbitrary one, for it is bound by the fact that in representing we think of what is represented and think it through by
dissecting it, by taking it apart and putting it together again.
But in thinking we not only place something before ourselves,
we not only dismember it for the sake of dismembering, but,
reflecting, we pursue the thing represented. We do not simply
accept it as it happens to fall to us; no, we undertake, as we
say, to get behind the thing. We find out how it stands with
the thing in general. We get an idea of it. We seek the universal.

From these listed characteristics of what we commonly call
"thinking," we shall for the present single out three:

1. Re-presentation "of our own accord"—considered as a
uniquely free act.

2. Re-presentation as analytical synthesis.

3. Grasp of the universal through re-presentation.

According to the sphere in which this re-presentation moves,
according to the degree of freedom, the sharpness and sureness of the analysis, and the breadth of its scope, thinking is
superficial or profound, empty or meaningful, irresponsible
or compelling, playful or serious.

But all this does not tell us, without further inquiry, why
thinking should enter into the fundamental relation to being,
indicated above. Along with desiring, willing, and feeling,

thinking is one of our capacities. Not only thinking but all our abilities and modes of behavior relate to the essent. Very true. But the differentiation between being and thinking involves something more essential than a mere relation to the essent. The differentiation springs from an initial inner union between thinking and being itself. The formula "being and thinking" designates a differentiation that is demanded as it were by being itself.

To be sure, such an inner union between thinking and being cannot be inferred from what we have so far said about thinking. Why not? Because we have not yet gained an adequate concept of thinking. But where are we to find such a concept?

In asking this question we are speaking as though such a thing as "logic" had not been with us for centuries.

Logic is the science of thinking, the doctrine of the rules of thinking and the forms of thought. Moreover, it is the one philosophical discipline in which views of the world, the trends of Weltanschauung, play little or no part. Furthermore logic passes as a secure and reliable science. It has taught the same thing from time immemorial. One logician, it is true, will modify the structure and order of the various traditional doctrines; another will introduce additions from epistemology; still another will provide a psychological underpinning. But on the whole a gratifying agreement prevails. Logic relieves us of the need for any troublesome inquiry into the essence of thinking.

And yet—we should like to raise one question. What does "logic" mean? The name is an abbreviation for *epistēmē logikē*, the science of the *logos*. And *logos* here means statement. But logic is supposed to be the doctrine of thinking. Why then is it the science of statement?

Why is thinking determined by statement? This is by no means self-evident. Previously we discussed "thinking" without reference to statement and discourse. Reflection on the essence of thinking is accordingly of a very particular kind when it is undertaken as reflection on *logos* and becomes logic. "Logic" and "the logical" are not simply the only possible ways of defining thought. On the other hand, it was no accident that the doctrine of thinking should have become "logic."

Be that as it may, to invoke logic for purposes of delimiting the essence of thinking is a questionable approach if only because logic as such, and not merely some of its doctrines and theories, is questionable. For this reason "logic" must be put in quotes. We do so not because we wish to deny "the logical" (in the sense of straight thinking). In the service of thought we are trying precisely to penetrate the source from which the essence of thinking is determined, namely *alētheia* and *physis*, being as unconcealment, the very thing that has been lost by "logic."

Since when, we now ask, has there been this logic which still dominates our thinking and our discourse and which from an early day has contributed in large part to determining the grammatical view of language and the basic Western attitude toward language in general. When did the development of logic begin? It began when Greek philosophy was drawing to an end and becoming an affair of schools, organization, and technique. It began when *eon*, the being of the essent, was represented as *idea* and as such became the "object" of *epistēmē*. Logic arose in the curriculum of the Platonic-Aristotelian schools. Logic is an invention of schoolteachers, not of philosophers. Where philosophers took it up it was always under more fundamental impulsions, not in the interest of logic. And it is no accident that the decisive efforts toward overcoming traditional logic were made by three of the greatest German thinkers, Leibniz, Kant, and Hegel.

Logic was able to arise as an exposition of the formal structure and rules of thought only after the division between being and thinking had been effected and indeed, only after it had been effected in a particular way and in a particular direction. Consequently logic itself and its history can never throw adequate light on the essence and origin of this separation between being and thinking. Logic itself is in need of an explanation and foundation in regard to its own origin and its claim to provide the authoritative interpretation of thinking. The historical origin of logic as a school discipline and the particulars of its development do not concern us here. Still, we must consider the following questions:

1. Why was it possible and indeed necessary that such a thing as "logic" should arise in the Platonic school?

2. Why was this doctrine of thinking a doctrine of *logos* in the sense of statement?

3. What was the basis of the steadily increasing prestige of the logical, ultimately expressed in these words of Hegel: "The logical (is) the absolute form of truth and, what is more, it is also the pure truth itself." (*Enzykl.* § 19, WW, 6, 29.) It is in keeping with this dominant position of logic that Hegel consciously applied the name of "logic" to the discipline otherwise known as "metaphysics." His "science of logic" has nothing in common with the usual textbook on logic.

To think is *intelligere* in Latin. It is the business of the intellect. If we wish to combat intellectualism seriously, we must know our adversary, i.e. we must know that intellectualism is only an impoverished modern offshoot of a development long in the making, namely the position of priority gained by thought with the help of Western metaphysics. It is important to curtail the excrescences of present-day intellectualism. But this will not shake or even touch its position. The danger of a relapse into intellectualism persists precisely for those who wish to combat it. A campaign directed solely against present intellectualism lends a semblance of justification to those who advocate a proper use of the traditional intellect. They may not be intellectualists but they come from the same source. This spiritual conservativism, stemming partly from natural inertia and partly from conscious effort, has become the feeding ground of political reaction. The misinterpretation of thought and the abuse to which it leads can be overcome only by authentic thinking that goes back to the roots—and *by nothing else*. The renewal of such thinking requires a return to the question of the essential relation of thinking to being, and this means the unfolding of the question of being as such. To surpass the traditional logic does not mean elimination of thought and the domination of sheer feeling; it means more radical, stricter thinking, a thinking that is part and parcel of being.

After this general exposition of the differentiation between being and thinking, we now ask more concretely:

1. What is the nature of the original unity between being and thinking, between *physis* and *logos?*

2. How did the original separation between *logos* and *physis* come about?

3. How did a separate and distinct *logos* come to appear on the scene?

4. How did the *logos* (the "logical") become the essence of thinking?

5. How did this *logos* in the sense of reason and understanding achieve domination over being in the beginning of Greek philosophy?

In accordance with our six guiding principles (cf. above p. 80) we shall once more look into the historical, i.e. the essential, origins of this separation. If the separation between being and thinking was an essential, necessary separation, it must have been rooted in an original bond between them. Hence our inquiry into the origin of the separation is first and foremost an inquiry into the essential bond between thinking and being.

In historical terms the question is: what was the nature of this bond in the crucial beginnings of Western philosophy? How was thinking understood in the beginning? That the Greek doctrine of thinking should have become a doctrine of *logos*, "logic," gives us a hint. Indeed, we encounter an original relationship between being, *physis*, and *logos*. We must merely free ourselves from the notion that originally and fundamentally *logos* and *legein* signified thought, understanding, and reason. As long as we cling to this opinion and even go so far as to interpret *logos* in the light of logic as it later developed, our attempt to rediscover the beginning of Greek philosophy can lead to nothing but absurdities. Moreover, where this view is held, it never becomes clear 1) how *logos* could ever have been separated from the being of the essent; 2) why this *logos* had to determine the essence of thinking and bring it into opposition with being.

Let us turn at once to the decisive point and ask: What do *logos* and *legein* mean if not thought and to think? *Logos* means the word, discourse, and *legein* means to speak, as in dia-logue, mono-logue. But originally *logos* did not mean speech, discourse. Its fundamental meaning stands in no direct relation to language. *Legō, legein,* Latin *legere,* is the same as the German word "lesen" ⟨to gather, collect, read⟩: "Ähren lesen, Holz lesen, die Weinlese, die Auslese" ⟨to glean, to gather wood, the vintage, the cream of the crop⟩; "ein Buch lesen" ⟨to read a book⟩ is only a variant of "lesen" in the strict sense, which is: to put one thing with another, to bring together, in short, to gather; but at the same time the one is marked off against the other. That is how the Greek mathematicians used the word. A coin collection is not a mere quantity assembled any which way. In the term "analogy" we actually find both meanings side by side: the original meaning of "relation" and that of "speech," "discourse." But in connection with the word "analogy" we have almost ceased to think of "speaking," while conversely, in connection with *logos,* the Greeks had not yet begun to think necessarily of "discourse" and "speaking."

As an example of the original meaning of *legein* as to "gather," we may take a passage in Homer, *Odyssey* XXIV 106. Recognizing the slain suitors in the underworld, Agamemnon says: "Amphimedon, what disaster has brought you here under the black earth, all picked men and years-mates? If one were to gather (*lexaito*) the best men of a *polis,* one could make no other choice." ⟨Cf. the English translation of W. H. D. Rouse, New York, Mentor, 1949, p. 248.⟩ And in *Physics,* θ I, 252 a 13, Aristotle says: *taxis de pasa logos,* "all order has a character of bringing together."

We shall not yet ask how the word passed from its original meaning, which had nothing to do with speech and words, to the signification of "to say" and "discourse." Here we shall only recall that long after the noun *logos* had come to mean discourse and statement it retained its original meaning in the sense of "relation of the one to the other."

In thus considering the basic meaning of *logos,* collection, to collect, we have not made much progress in clarifying the question: in what way were being and *logos* originally united for the Greeks, so that they could subsequently separate and for definite reasons had to do so?

Reference to the basic meaning of *logos* can give us a hint only if we understand what "being" meant to the Greeks: namely *physis.* Not only have we tried to gain a general under-

standing of being as the Greeks saw it; we have circumscribed
it more and more closely through its delimitations over against
becoming and appearance.

Keeping all this in mind, we say: Being in the sense of
physis is the power that emerges. As contrasted with becoming, it is permanence, permanent presence. Contrasted with
appearance, it is appearing, manifest presence.

What has *logos* (collection) to do with being interpreted
in this way? But first we must ask: is there proof of any such
connection between being and *logos* at the beginning of Greek
philosophy? Yes, indeed. Again we go back to the two decisive thinkers, Parmenides and Heraclitus, and attempt once
more to gain admittance into the Greek world, whose foundations, even though distorted and transposed, covered and concealed, still sustain our world. Precisely because we have em-
barked on the great and long venture of demolishing a world
that has grown old and of rebuilding it authentically anew,
i.e. historically, we must know the tradition. We must know
more—i.e. our knowledge must be stricter and more binding
—than all the epochs before us, even the most revolutionary.
Only the most radical historical knowledge can make us aware
of our extraordinary tasks and preserve us from a new wave
of mere restoration and uncreative imitation.

We begin our proof of the inner bond between *logos* and
physis in the beginning of Western philosophy with an interpretation of Heraclitus.

Of all the early Greek thinkers it is Heraclitus who, in the
course of Western history, has suffered the most transformation along un-Greek lines, and yet who in recent years has provided the strongest impulse toward rediscovery of the authentic Greek spirit. Hegel and Hölderlin were both under the
great and fruitful spell of Heraclitus, but with the difference
that Hegel looked backward and drew a line under the past
while Hölderlin looked forward and opened up the way to
the future. Still different was Nietzsche's relation to Heraclitus.
Nietzsche was a victim of the current (and false) opposition
between Parmenides and Heraclitus. This is one of the main
reasons why in his metaphysics he did not find his way to the
decisive question, even though he understood the great age

of Greek beginnings with a depth that was surpassed only by Hölderlin.

Christianity was responsible for the misinterpretation of Heraclitus. It was begun by the Old Church Fathers. Hegel was still in this tradition. Heraclitus' doctrine of the logos* was regarded as the forerunner of the logos that figures in the New Testament—in the prologue to the Gospel of St. John. The logos is Christ. But Heraclitus already spoke of the logos and this meant that the Greeks had reached the very gates of the absolute truth, namely the revealed truth of Christianity. In a book that came to me only a few days ago I read: "The real appearance of truth in the form of the God-man set the seal on the Greeks' philosophical insight concerning the rule of the logos over all existence. This confirmation and seal establish the classicism of Greek philosophy."

According to this widespread interpretation of history the Greeks are the classics of philosophy, because they were not yet full-grown Christian theologians. But we shall first listen to Heraclitus himself before deciding what to think of him as a forerunner of Christianity.

We begin with two fragments in which Heraclitus speaks expressly of the *logos*. In our version we intentionally leave the crucial word *logos* untranslated, for we hope to gain its meaning from the context.

Fragment 1: But while the *logos* remains always this, men remain uncomprehending (*axynetoi*), both before they have heard and just after they have heard. For everything becomes essent in accordance with this *logos*, *kata ton logon tonde;* but they (men) resemble those who have never in their experience ventured anything, although they try their hand at words and works such as I perform, separating all things *kata physin,* according to being, and explaining how they behave. As to the other men (the other men as they all are, *hoi polloi*), from them what they actually do when awake is hidden, just as what they have done in sleep is hidden from them afterward.

* "Logos" is italic where Heidegger used Greek, roman where he transliterated. R.M.

Fragment 2: Therefore it is necessary to follow it, i.e. to adhere to togetherness in the essent; but though the *logos* is this togetherness in the essent, the many live as though each had his own understanding (opinion).

What do these two fragments tell us?

It is said that 1) permanence and endurance are characteristic of the *logos;* 2) it is togetherness in the essent, the togetherness of all essents, that which gathers; 3) everything that happens, i.e. that comes into being, stands there in accordance with this permanent togetherness; this is the dominant power.

What is said here of *logos* corresponds exactly to the actual meaning of the word "collection" ⟨Sammlung⟩. But just as the German word means 1) collecting and 2) collectedness, so *logos* means here collecting collectedness, the primal gathering principle. *Logos* here signifies neither meaning nor word nor doctrine, and surely not "meaning of a doctrine"; it means: the original collecting collectedness which is in itself permanently dominant.

In Fragment 1, to be sure, the context seems to suggest an interpretation in the sense of word and discourse, and even to demand it as the only possible explanation; for it speaks of the "hearing" of men. There is a fragment (50) in which this connection between *logos* and "hearing" is directly expressed: "If you have heard not me but the *logos,* then it is wise to say accordingly: all is one." Here the *logos* is assuredly taken as something "audible." What else can this word mean but statement, discourse, word? Particularly since at Heraclitus' time *legein* was already current in the meaning of "to speak."

Heraclitus himself says (Fragment 73): "We must not act and speak as if asleep." Here *legein* in opposition to *poiein* can obviously mean nothing other than to speak. And nevertheless, in the crucial passages cited above (Fragments 1 and 2) *logos* means not discourse and not word. Fragment 50, which seems particularly to argue for *logos* as discourse, suggests an entirely different perspective if properly interpreted.

In order to see and understand what *logos* means in the

sense of "permanent gathering" we must take a closer look at the context of the first two fragments.

In confronting the *logos*, men are uncomprehending (*axynetoi*)—they do not comprehend the *logos*. Heraclitus uses this word frequently (see particularly Fragment 34). It is the negation of *syniēmi* which signifies "bring together": *axynetoi;* that is to say, men are those who do not bring together . . . what do they not bring together? the *logos, that which is permanently together,* collectedness. Men are those who do not bring it together, who do not comprehend it, who do not compass it in one, and this regardless of whether or not they have heard it. The next sentence makes the meaning clear. Men do not penetrate to the *logos* even if they attempt to do so with words, *epea*. Here indeed word and discourse are mentioned, but they are differentiated from, and even opposed to, *logos*. Heraclitus means to say: Men have hearing, they hear words, but in this hearing, they cannot "heed," i.e. follow what is not audible like words, what is not a *discourse,* a *speaking,* but indeed the *logos*. Thus, properly understood, Fragment 50 proves the exact opposite of what is read into it. It says: do not attach importance to words but heed the *logos*. Because *logos* and *legein* already signified discourse and to speak, but since these are not the essence of the *logos*, *logos* here is opposed to *epea*, discourse. Correspondingly, the hearing that is a following ⟨Hörig-sein⟩ is contrasted with mere hearing. Mere hearing scatters and diffuses itself in what is commonly believed and said, in hearsay, in *doxa*, appearance. True hearing has nothing to do with ear and mouth, but means: to follow the *logos* and what it is, namely the collectedness of the essent itself. We can hear truly only if we are followers. But this has nothing to do with the lobes of our ears. The man who is no follower is removed and excluded from the *logos* from the start, regardless of whether he has heard with his ears or not yet heard. Those who merely hear by listening around and assembling rumors are and remain the *axynetoi*, the uncomprehending. They are described in Fragment 34: "Those who do not bring together the permanent togetherness hear but resemble the deaf." They hear words and speeches but they are closed to what they should give heed to. As the proverb says, they are: Present yet absent.

But in regard to what are most men present and at the same time absent? Fragment 72 gives the answer: "For what they associate with most closely, the *logos*, to it they turn their back; and what they encounter every day seems strange to them."

Men are forever with the *logos*, yet forever removed from it, absent though present; thus they are the *axynetoi*, those who do not comprehend.

Wherein consists then men's inability to grasp and comprehend, when they hear words but do not grasp the *logos*? What is it that they are with and yet absent from? Men have always to do with being in that they are always dealing with essents; it is alien to them in that they turn away from being, because they do not grasp it but suppose that essents are only essents and nothing more. They are awake (in relation to the essent) and yet being is hidden from them. They sleep and even their actions pass from them. They thrash about amid the essents, always supposing that what is most tangible is what they must grasp, and thus each man grasps what is closest to him. The one holds to this, the other to that, each man's opinion ⟨ Sinn ⟩ hinges on his own ⟨ eigen ⟩; it is opinionatedness ⟨ Eigen-sinn ⟩. This opinionatedness, this obstinacy, prevents them from reaching out to what is gathered together in itself, makes it impossible for them to be followers ⟨ Hörige ⟩ and to hear ⟨ hören ⟩ accordingly.

Logos is the steady gathering, the intrinsic togetherness of the essent, i.e. being. Therefore in Fragment 1 *kata ton logon* means the same as *kata physin*. *Physis* and *logos* are the same. *Logos* characterizes being in a new and yet old respect: that which is, which stands straight and distinct in itself, is at the same time gathered togetherness in itself and by itself, and maintains itself in such togetherness. *Eon*, beingness, is essentially *xynon*, collected presence; *xynon* does not mean the "universal" but that which in itself collects all things and holds them together. According to Fragment 114, such a *xynon* is, for example, the *nomos* for the *polis*, the statute that constitutes or puts together, the inner structure of the *polis*, not a universal, not something that hovers over all and touches none, but the original unifying unity of what tends apart. The opinionatedness, *idia phronēsis*, for which the *logos* is sealed, attaches itself only to the one or the other side and supposes that it has captured the truth. Fragment 103 says: "Gathered together, the beginning and end of the circle are the same." It would be absurd to interpret *xynon* here as the "universal."

To the opinionated life is only life; death is death and only death. But life's being is also death. Everything that enters into life also begins to die, to go toward its death, and death is at the same time life. Heraclitus says in Fragment 8: "Opposites move back and forth, the one to the other; from out of themselves they gather themselves." The conflict of the opposites is a gathering, rooted in togetherness, it is *logos*. The being of the essents is the supreme radiance, i.e. the greatest beauty, that which is most permanent in itself. What the Greeks meant by "beauty" was restraint. The gathering of the supreme antagonism is *polemos*, struggle (as we have seen above) in the sense of setting apart ⟨ Aus-einandersetzung ⟩. For us moderns, on the contrary, the beautiful is what reposes and relaxes; it is intended for enjoyment and art is a matter for pastry cooks. It makes no essential difference whether the enjoyment of art serves to satisfy the sensibilities of the connoisseur and esthete or to provide moral edification. For the Greeks *on* and *kalon* meant the same thing (presence was pure radiance). The esthetic view is very different; it is as old as logic. For esthetics art is representation of the beautiful in the sense of the pleasing, the pleasant. But art is disclosure of the being of the essent. On the strength of a recaptured, pristine, relation to being we must provide the word "art" with a new content.

We conclude our characterization of the logos as Heraclitus thought it, with two points that still preserve their full force.

1. There can be true speaking and hearing only if they are directed in advance toward being, the logos. Only where the logos discloses itself does the phonetic sound become a word. Only where the being of the essent is heard does a mere casual listening become a hearing. But those who do not grasp the *logos, akousai ouk epistamenoi oud' eipein,* "are not able to hear or to speak" (Fragment 19). They cannot bring their being-there to stand in the being of the essent. Only those who can do so master the word; these are the poets and thinkers. The others stagger about in their obstinacy and ignorance.

They recognize only what runs across their path, what pleases them and is familiar to them. They are like dogs: *kynes gar kai bauzousin hōn an mē gignōskōsi*, "for the dogs bark at everyone they do not know" (Fragment 97). They are donkeys: *onous syrmat' an helesthai mallon ē chryson.* "Donkeys prefer chaff to gold" (Fragment 9). Always and everywhere they deal with essents. But being remains hidden from them. Being is not tangible, it cannot be heard with the ears or smelled. Being is anything but vapor and smoke: *ei panta ta onta kapnos genoito, rhines an diagnoen.* "If all essents went up in smoke, it is the noses that would differentiate and apprehend them" (Fragment 7).

2. Because being as logos is basic gathering, not mass and turmoil in which everything has as much or as little value as everything else, rank and domination are implicit in being. If being is to disclose itself, it must itself have and maintain a rank. That is why Heraclitus spoke of the many as dogs and donkeys. This attitude was an essential part of Greek being-there. Nowadays a little too much fuss is sometimes made over the Greek polis. If one is going to concern oneself with the polis, this aspect should not be forgotten, or else the whole idea becomes insignificant and sentimental. What has the higher rank is the stronger. Therefore being, the logos as gathering and harmony, is not easily accessible and not accessible to all in the same form; unlike the harmony that is mere compromise, destruction of tension, flattening, it is hidden: *harmoniē aphanēs phanerēs kreittōn*, "the harmony that does not (immediately and easily) show itself is mightier than that which is (at all times) manifest" (Fragment 54).

Because being is *logos, harmonia, alētheia, physis, phainesthai*, it does not show itself as one pleases. The true is not for every man but only for the strong. It is with a view to this inner superiority and hiddenness of being that Heraclitus spoke those strange words which, because they are seemingly so un-Greek, bear witness to the Greek experience of the being of the essent: *all hōsper sarma eikē kechumenon ho kallistos kosmos.* "The most beautiful world is like a heap of rubble, tossed down in confusion" (Fragment 124).

Sarma is the antithesis of *logos*, that which is merely tossed down over against that which stands in itself, muddle over against togetherness, unbeing over against being.

The popular interpretation of Heraclitus tends to sum up his philosophy in the dictum *panta rhei*, "everything flows." *If* these words stem from Heraclitus to begin with, they do not mean that everything is mere continuous and evanescent change, pure impermanence; no, they mean that the essent as a whole, in its being, is hurled back and forth from one opposition to another; being is the gathering of this conflict and unrest.

If we take the basic meaning of *logos* as gathering and togetherness, we must note the following:

Gathering is never a mere driving-together and heaping-up. It maintains in a common bond the conflicting and that which tends apart. It does not let them fall into haphazard dispersion. In thus maintaining a bond, the *logos* has the character of permeating power, of *physis*. It does not let what it holds in its power dissolve into an empty freedom from opposition, but by uniting the opposites maintains the full sharpness of their tension.

Here is the place to return briefly to the Christian concept of the logos, particularly as it appears in the New Testament. For a more detailed exposition we should have to distinguish between the Synoptic Gospels and the Gospel of St. John. But in principle we may say this: logos in the New Testament does not, as in Heraclitus, mean the being of the essent, the gathering together of the conflicting; it means *one* particular essent, namely the son of God. And specifically it refers to him in the role of mediator between God and men. This New Testament notion of the logos is that of the Jewish philosophy of religion developed by Philo whose doctrine of creation attributes to the logos the function of *mesitēs*, the mediator. How so? Because in the Greek translation of the Old Testament (Septuagint) *logos* signifies the word, and what is more, the "word" in the definite meaning of command and commandment; *hoi deka logoi* are the ten commandments of God (decalogue). Thus *logos* signifies the *kēryx*, the *angelos*, the herald, the messenger, who hands down commands and commandments; *logos tou staurou* is the word of the cross. The proclamation of the cross is Christ himself; he is the logos of redemption, of eternal life, *logos zōēs*. A whole world separates all this from Heraclitus.

We have attempted to set forth the essential bond between *logos* and *physis*—for on the basis of this unity we mean to show the inner necessity and possibility of the separation between them.

But at this point an objection seems to arise against this characterization of the Heraclitean logos: if logos and being are so intimately and essentially linked, how, one wonders, can this unity and identity of *physis* and *logos* give rise to the opposition between being and thought as logos? Assuredly this is a question, a question which we do not mean to make too easy for ourselves, although there is a great temptation to do so. For the present we may only say this: If the unity of *physis* and *logos* is so fundamental, the separation between them must be just as much so. If in addition this distinction between being and thinking is different in kind and direction from the preceding distinctions, it must also have arisen in a different way. Therefore, just as we have striven to keep our interpretation of *logos* free from all later falsifications and to understand it through the essence of *physis*, we must also endeavor to understand the separation of *physis* and *logos* in a purely Greek way, i.e. on the basis of *physis* and *logos*. For in considering the separation and opposition of *physis* and *logos*, of being and thinking, we are exposed to an almost more persistent danger of modern falsification than in considering their unity. How so?

In defining the opposition between being and thinking, we move in a familiar schema. Being is the objective, the object. Thinking is the subjective, the subject. The relation of thinking to being is that of subject to object. The Greeks, it is supposed, conceived this relation in an extremely primitive way, for this was the beginning of philosophy and they lacked training in epistemology. A further supposition is that there is nothing in the opposition between being and thinking to demand reflection. And yet we must *inquire*.

What is the essential law governing the separation of *physis* and *logos*? In order to disclose this law we must conceive the bond between *logos* and *physis*, their unity, more sharply than before. This we shall attempt to do with the help of Parmenides. We do so advisedly because the current opinion is that however the doctrine of the logos may be interpreted it is peculiar to the philosophy of Heraclitus.

Parmenides stood on the same ground as Heraclitus. Where indeed would we expect these two Greek thinkers, the inaugurators of all philosophy, to stand if not in the being of the essent? For Parmenides, too, being was *hen, syneches,* holding together in itself; *mounon,* unique and unifying; *houlon,* complete and fully-standing—the permanently manifested power through which shines perpetually the appearance of the one-and-many-sided. Hence the indispensable way to being is threefold and leads through unconcealment.

But where does Parmenides speak of the *logos,* not to mention what we are now seeking, the separation between being and the logos? If we find anything whatever in this respect, it would seem to be the very opposite of a divergence. There is one proposition that has come down to us in two versions. Fragment 5 puts it thus: *to gar auto noein estin te kai einai.* The crude translation prescribed by a long tradition runs: "Thinking and being are the same"—a misinterpretation no less un-Greek than the falsification of the Heraclitean doctrine of the logos.

Noein is understood as thinking, an activity of the subject. The thinking of the subject determines what being is. Being is nothing other than the object of thinking, that which is thought. But since thinking remains a subjective activity, and since thinking and being are supposed to be the same according to Parmenides, everything becomes subjective. Nothing is in itself. But such a doctrine, we are told, is found in Kant and the German idealists. Essentially Parmenides anticipated their teachings. He is much praised for this progressive achievement, particularly in comparison with Aristotle, a later Greek thinker. Over against the idealism of Plato, Aristotle advocated a variety of realism and was therefore the precursor of the Middle Ages.

This familiar German view requires special mention here, not only because it works its mischief in all historical accounts of Greek philosophy, not only because recent philosophers have interpreted the early history of philosophy in this way, but above all because the dominance of these views has made it difficult for us to understand the authentic truth of the primordially Greek words spoken by Parmenides. It is only by understanding them that we shall be able to appraise the change that has taken place, not only in the modern era but beginning with late antiquity and the rise of Christianity—a change that has affected the whole spiritual history of the West, that is to say, its history pure and simple.

To gar auto noein estin te kai einai. In order to understand this sentence we must know three things:

1. What is the meaning of *to auto* and *te kai?*
2. What is the meaning of *noein?*
3. What is the meaning of *einai?*

In regard to the third question we seem sufficiently informed by what has been said about *physis* in the foregoing. But *noein* is obscure unless we simply translate it as "thinking" and define it, in the logical sense, as analytic statement. *Noein* means vernehmen ⟨ to apprehend ⟩, *nous* means Vernehmung ⟨ apprehension ⟩,* this in two senses that belong together. To apprehend means to accept, to let something (namely that which shows itself, which appears) come to one. Vernehmen means also to hear a witness, to question him and so determine the facts, to establish how a matter stands. To apprehend ⟨ Vernehmen ⟩ in this twofold sense means to let something come to one, not merely accepting it, however, but taking a receptive attitude toward that which shows itself. When troops prepare to receive the enemy, it is in the hope of stopping him at the very least, of bringing him to stand ⟨ zum Stehen bringen ⟩. This receptive bringing-to-stand is meant in *noein*. It is this apprehension that Parmenides says to be the same as being. This brings us to a clarification of our first question: What is the meaning of *to auto*, the same?

For us two things that are the same are interchangeable,

---

* Here I have cited the German words first in order to indicate that in the following, and to the end of the present translation, "apprehend" and "apprehension" are used exclusively to render vernehmen and Vernehmung as defined in this passage by Heidegger. Dictionary renderings of vernehmen are: to hear, to perceive, to understand, to learn, to interrogate. I have chosen "apprehend" only because it is less weighted with popular meaning and hence perhaps more amenable to Heidegger's definition of "vernehmen." R.M.

one and the same. What sort of unity is meant in this self-sameness? We cannot determine this as we please. Here, in speaking of "being," the unity must be understood as Parmenides understood the word *hen*. We know that this unity is never empty indifference; it is not sameness in the sense of mere equivalence. Unity is the belonging-together of antagonisms. This is original oneness.

Why does Parmenides say *te kai*? Because being and thinking in a contending sense are one, i.e. the same in the sense of belonging-together. How are we to understand this? Let us start from being, which as *physis* has become clearer to us in several respects. Being means: to stand in the light, to appear, to enter into unconcealment. Where this happens, i.e. where being prevails, apprehension prevails and happens with it; the two belong together. Apprehension is the receptive bringing-to-stand of the intrinsically permanent that manifests itself.

Parmenides states the same proposition still more sharply in Fragment 8, line 34: *Tauton d'esti noein te kai houneken esti noēma.* The same is apprehension and that for the sake of which apprehension occurs. Apprehension occurs for the sake of being. There is being only when there is appearing, entering into unconcealment, when unconcealment occurs, when there is disclosure. In these two versions Parmenides gives us a still more fundamental insight into the essence of *physis.* To it *belongs* apprehension, which shares in its power.

At first sight the statement says nothing about man, still less about man as subject, and nothing whatever about a subject which cancels out everything objective, transforming it into mere subjectivity. The proposition says the opposite of all this: being dominates, but because and insofar as it dominates and appears, appearing and *with* it apprehension must *also* occur. But if man is to participate in this appearing and apprehension, he must himself be, he must belong to being. But then the essence and the mode of being-human can only be determined by the essence of being.

But if appearing belongs to being as *physis*, then man as an essent must belong to this appearing. Since being-human amid the essent as a whole is evidently a particular mode of being, the particularity of being-human will grow from the particularity of its belonging to being as dominant appearing. And since apprehension—accepting apprehension of what shows itself—belongs to such appearing, it may be presumed that this is precisely what determines the essence of being-human. Thus, in interpreting Parmenides' proposition, we must not read some later idea, and above all not a present-day idea, of being-human into it. Quite on the contrary, it is the proposition itself that must tell us how, according to *it*, and that is, according to the essence of being, being-human is determined.

According to Heraclitus what man is is first manifested (*edeixe,* shows itself) in *polemos,* in the separation of gods and men, in the irruption of being itself. For philosophy what man is is not written somewhere in heaven. We must rather say:

1. The determination of the essence of man is *never* an answer but essentially a question.

2. The asking of this question and the decision in this question are historical, and not merely in a general sense; no, this question is the very essence of history.

3. The question of what man is must always be taken in its essential bond with the question of how it stands with being. The question of man is not an anthropological question but a historically meta-physical question. [The question cannot be adequately asked in the domain of traditional metaphysics which remains essentially "physics."]

Consequently we must not misinterpret *nous* and *noein* in this proposition of Parmenides according to a concept of man supplied by us, but must learn that man's being is determined by the essential belonging-together of being and apprehension.

What is man where being and apprehension reign? The beginning of Fragment 6, which is already known to us, gives us the answer: *Chrē to legein te noein t'eon emmenai.* Both are needful, the *legein* as well as the apprehension—of the essent in its being.

Noein may not yet be interpreted as thinking. Nor does it suffice to consider it as Vernehmung if we take the usual unwitting view of "Vernehmung" as an activity of man, of a man whom we conceive in accordance with a pale and empty biology and psychology or epistemology. And this occurs even when we do not specifically invoke such conceptions.

Apprehension, as Parmenides says, is not a faculty belonging to a man already defined; apprehension is rather a process in which man first enters into history as a being, an essent, i.e. (in the literal sense) comes into being.

Apprehension is not a function that man has as an attribute, but rather the other way around: apprehension is the happening that has man. That is why Parmenides always speaks simply of *noein*, of apprehension. What is accomplished in this maxim is nothing less than the knowing appearance of man as historical being (as the historical custodian of being). This, for the West, is the crucial definition of being-human, and at the same time it embodies an essential characterization of being. The separation between being and being-human comes to light in their togetherness. We can no longer discern this separation through the pale and empty dichotomy of "being and thinking" which lost its roots hundreds of years ago, unless we go back to its beginnings.

The mode and direction of the opposition between being and thinking are so unique because it is here that man comes face to face with being. This event marks the knowing emergence of man as the historical being. It is only after man became known as the historical essent that he was "defined" in a concept, namely as the *zōion logon echon*, the rational animal. In this definition of man the *logos* occurs, but in a totally unrecognizable form and in very odd company.

This definition of man is fundamentally a zoological one. The *zōion* of this zoology is in many respects questionable. But the Western doctrine of man—all psychology, ethics, theory of knowledge and anthropology—has been filled into the frame of *this* definition. For years we have been thrashing around in a confused mixture of ideas and concepts drawn from these disciplines.

But since the definition of man supporting the whole structure was in itself a degeneration—not to mention the interpretation that was put on it later—we shall see nothing of what is said, and of what happens in Parmenides' maxim, as long as we think and inquire along the lines laid down by this definition.

But the current conception of man in all its variants is only one of the barriers that cut us off from the realm where the manifestation of being-human first occurred and was first stabilized. The other barrier is that even the so-called *question* concerning man remains alien to us.

To be sure, there are books today entitled: "What is man?" But the title merely stands in letters on the cover. There is no questioning. Not only because people have been so busy writing books that they have forgotten how to question, but because the writers already possess an answer and what is more an answer that forbids questioning. If a man believes the propositions of Catholic dogma, that is his individual concern; we shall not discuss it here. But how can we be expected to take a man seriously who writes "What is man?" on the cover of his book although he does *not* inquire, because he is *un*willing and *un*able to inquire. And when the *Frankfurter Zeitung*, among others, praises such a book, which questions merely on its cover, as "an extraordinary, magnificent and courageous work," even the blindest among us know where we stand.

Why do I speak of such irrelevancies in connection with the exegesis of Parmenides' dictum? In itself this sort of scribbling is unimportant and insignificant. What is not unimportant is the paralysis of all passion for questioning that has long been with us. The consequence of this paralysis is that all standards and perspectives have been confused and that most men have ceased to know where and between what the crucial decisions must be made, if a sharp and original historical knowledge is to be combined with greatness of historical will. Such hints as we have thrown out can only suggest how far questioning as a fundamental element of historical being has receded from us. But we have even lost our understanding for the question. For this reason let us set forth the essential points that must be borne in mind if we are to think through the ensuing argument:

1. The determination of the essence of man is never an answer but essentially a question.

2. The asking of this question is historical in the fundamental sense that this questioning first creates history.

3. This is so because the question as to what man is can only be asked as part of the inquiry about being.

4. Only where being discloses itself in questioning does history happen and with it the being of man, by virtue of which he ventures to set himself apart from the essent as such and contend ⟨ auseinandersetzen ⟩ with it.

5. It is questioning contending that first brings man back to the essent that he himself is and must be.

6. Only as a questioning, historical being does man come to himself; only as such is he a self. Man's selfhood means this: he must transform the being that discloses itself to him into history and bring himself to stand in it. Selfhood does not mean that he is primarily an "ego" and an individual. This he is no more than he is a we, a community.

7. Because man as a historical being is himself, the question about his own being must be reformulated. Rather than "What is man?" we should say "Who is man?"

What is expressed in Parmenides' maxim is a definition of the essence of man from out of the essence of being itself.

We still do not know how the essence of man is here defined. It was first necessary to mark off the realm in which Parmenides speaks and which in speaking he helps to disclose. But these general pointers do not suffice to free us from the current notions of man and the current concepts in which he is defined. In order to understand the maxim, in order to grasp its truth, we must gain some positive idea of Greek being-there and Greek being.

From the Heraclitean fragment several times quoted we know that the separation between gods and men took place only in *polemos,* in the conflict which sets (being) apart. It is only such conflict that *edeixe,* that *shows,* that brings forth gods and men in their being. We do not learn who man is by learned definitions; we learn it only when man contends with the essent, striving to bring it into its being, i.e. into limit and form, that is to say when he projects something new (not yet present), when he creates original poetry, when he builds poetically.

The thinking of Parmenides and Heraclitus was still poetic, which in this case means philosophical and not scientific. But

because in this poetic thinking the thinking has priority, the
thought about man's being follows its own direction and proportions. This poetic thinking forms a body with the contrary
aspect, the thinking poetry of the Greeks and particularly that
poetry in which the being and (closely related) being-there
of the Greeks was in the truest sense created: the tragedy. Let
us consult the tragedy for a better understanding of Greek poetic philosophy.

We are seeking to understand the origin of the differentiation between "being and thinking." This differentiation is a
name for the fundamental attitude of the Western spirit. In
accordance with this attitude, being is defined from the standpoint of thinking and reason. This is true even where the Western spirit shuns the domination of reason by seeking the "ir-
rational" and "alogical."

In our quest for the source of the differentiation between
"being and thinking" we have come across Parmenides'
maxim: *to gar auto noein estin te kai einai.* According to the
usual translation and interpretation it means: Thinking and
being are the same.

We may call this maxim the guiding principle of Western
philosophy, but only if we append this note to it:

The maxim became the guiding principle of Western philosophy only when it ceased to be understood because its
original truth could not be held fast. The falling away from
the truth of this maxim began with the Greeks themselves,
immediately after Parmenides. Men can retain basic truths
of such magnitude only by raising them continuously to a
still more original unfolding; not merely by applying them
and invoking their authority. The original remains original
only if it never loses the possibility of being what it is: origin
as emergence (from the concealment of the essence). We are
trying to regain the basic and original truth of the maxim. We
have given the first hint of a different interpretation by our
translation. The maxim does not say: "Thinking and being
are the same." It says: "There is a reciprocal bond between
apprehension and being."

But what does this mean?

In one way or another it is man who speaks in this maxim.

Hence it is almost inevitable that the prevailing idea of man should be carried into the maxim.

But this produces a falsification of the essence of man as experienced by the Greeks, according either to the Christian or to the modern concept of man, or else according to a pale and diluted mixture of the two.

But this misinterpretation in the direction of a non-Greek notion of man is the lesser evil.

The real catastrophe is to be sought in a total failure to understand the truth of the maxim.

For in this maxim the crucial definition of being-human was accomplished. Hence in interpreting it we must avoid not only all inappropriate ideas of man but all ideas of man whatsoever. We must attempt to hear only what is said.

But because we are inexperienced at such hearing, and because moreover our ears are full of things that prevent us from hearing properly, it has been necessary to state the conditions for a proper inquiry as to who man is—though we have done little more than list them.

And because the definition of being-human effected by Parmenides is strange and hard to approach directly, we shall first seek help and counsel by consulting the poetic project of being-human among the Greeks.

We read the first chorus from the Antigone of Sophocles (lines 332–75). First we listen to the Greek words in order to get some of the sound into our ears. The translation runs:

There is much that is strange, but nothing
that surpasses man in strangeness.
He sets sail on the frothing waters
amid the south winds of winter
tacking through the mountains
and furious chasms of the waves.
He wearies even the noblest
of the gods, the Earth,
indestructible and untiring,
overturning her from year to year,
driving the plows this way and that
with horses.

And man, pondering and plotting,
snares the light-gliding birds
and hunts the beasts of the wilderness
and the native creatures of the sea.
With guile he overpowers the beast
that roams the mountains by night as by day,
he yokes the hirsute neck of the stallion
and the undaunted bull.

And he has found his way
to the resonance of the word,
and to wind-swift all-understanding,
and to the courage of rule over cities.
He has considered also how to flee
from exposure to the arrows
of unpropitious weather and frost.

Everywhere journeying, inexperienced and without issue,
he comes to nothingness.
Through no flight can he resist
the one assault of death,
even if he has succeeded in cleverly evading
painful sickness.

Clever indeed, mastering
the ways of skill beyond all hope,
he sometimes accomplishes evil,
sometimes achieves brave deeds.
He wends his way between the laws of the earth
and the adjured justice of the gods.
Rising high above his place,
he who for the sake of adventure takes
the nonessent for essent loses
his place in the end.

May such a man never frequent my hearth;
May my mind never share the presumption
of him who does this.

The following commentary is necessarily inadequate, if only
because it cannot be built up from the poet's entire work or

even from the whole tragedy. Here I shall not be able to go into the choice of readings or the changes that have been made in the text. Our interpretation falls into *three phases*, in each of which we shall consider the whole poem from a different point of view.

In the first phase we shall set forth the intrinsic meaning of the poem, that which sustains the edifice of words and rises above it.

In the second phase we pass through the whole sequence of strophes and antistrophes and delimit the area that is opened up by the poem.

In the third phase we attempt to take our stand in the center of the poem, with a view to judging who man is according to this poetic discourse.

First phase. We seek that which sustains the whole and towers above it. Actually we have not far to seek. It is threefold; it bursts upon us like a triple assault, shattering at the very outset all everyday standards of questioning and definition.

The first is the beginning:

> There is much that is strange, but nothing
> that surpasses man in strangeness.

In these first two verses the poet anticipates. He will spend the rest of the poem in catching up with himself. Man, in *one* word, is *deinotaton*, the strangest. This one word encompasses the extreme limits and abrupt abysses of his being. This aspect of the ultimate and abysmal can never be discerned through the mere description that establishes data, even though thousands of eyes should examine man, searching for attributes and states. Such being is disclosed only to poetic insight. We find no portrayal of existing specimens of man; nor do we find any sort of blind and fatuous inflation of human essence from below, inspired by peevish yearning for some unattained glory; here there is no suggestion of a pre-eminent personality. Among the Greeks there were no personalities (and for this reason no supra-personality). Man is *to deinotaton*, the strangest of the strange. Here we must anticipate an explanation of the Greek word *deinon* and of our translation. This calls for a tacit glance over the whole poem, which alone can provide an appropriate interpretation of the first two verses. The Greek word *deinon* has the strange ambiguity with which Greek discourse cuts across the contending separations 〈 Aus-einander-setzungen 〉 of being.

On the one hand *deinon* means the terrible, but not in the sense of petty terrors, and above all not in the decadent, insipid, and useless sense that the word has taken on today, in such locutions as "terribly cute." The *deinon* is the terrible in the sense of the overpowering power which compels panic fear, true fear; and in equal measure it is the collected, silent awe that vibrates with its own rhythm. The mighty, the overpowering is the essential character of power itself. Where it irrupts, it *can* hold its overpowering power in check. Yet this does not make it more innocuous, but *still* more terrible and remote.

But on the other hand *deinon* means the powerful in the sense of one who uses power, who not only disposes of power 〈 Gewalt 〉 but is violent 〈 gewalt-tätig 〉 insofar as the use of power is the basic trait not only of his action but also of his being-there. Here we use the word violence in an essential sense extending beyond the common usage of the word, as mere arbitrary brutality. In this common usage violence is seen from the standpoint of a realm which draws its standards from conventional compromise and mutual aid, and which accordingly disparages all violence as a disturbance of the peace.

The essent as a whole, seen as power, is the overpowering, *deinon* in the first sense. Man is *deinon*, first because he remains exposed within this overpowering power, because by his essence he belongs to being. But at the same time man is *deinon* because he is the violent one in the sense designated above. (He gathers the power and brings it to manifestness.) Man is the violent one, not aside from and along with other attributes but solely in the sense that in his fundamental violence 〈 Gewalt-tätigkeit 〉 he uses power 〈 Gewalt 〉 against the overpowering 〈 Überwältigende 〉. Because he is twice *deinon* in a sense that is originally one, he is *to deinotaton*, the most powerful: violent in the midst of the overpowering.

But why do we translate *deinon* as "strange" 〈 unheimlich 〉? Not in order to hide or attenuate the meaning of powerful, overpowering, violent; quite on the contrary. Because this *deinon* is meant as the supreme limit and link of man's being, the essence of the being thus defined should from the first be seen in its crucial aspect. But, in that case, is the designation of the powerful as the strange and uncanny ⟨ unheimlich ⟩ not a posterior notion derived from the impression that the powerful makes on us, whereas the essential here is to understand the *deinon* as what it intrinsically is? That is so, but we are not taking the strange in the sense of an impression on our states of feeling.

We are taking the strange, the uncanny ⟨ das Unheimliche ⟩, as that which casts us out of the "homely," i.e. the customary, familiar, secure. The unhomely ⟨ Unheimische ⟩ prevents us from making ourselves at home and therein it is overpowering. But man is the strangest of all, not only because he passes his life amid the strange understood in this sense but because he departs from his customary, familiar limits, because he is the violent one, who, tending toward the strange in the sense of the overpowering, surpasses the limit of the familiar ⟨ das Heimische ⟩.

To understand the full implication of these words of the chorus, we must bear this in mind: to say that man is *to deinotaton*, the strangest of all, is not to impute a particular attribute to man, as though he were also something else; no, the verse says that to be the strangest of all is the basic trait of the human essence, within which all other traits must find their place. In calling man "the strangest of all" it gives the authentic Greek definition of man. We shall fully appreciate this phenomenon of strangeness only if we experience the power of appearance and the struggle with it as an essential part of being-there.

The second passage that sustains the poetic edifice and rises above it is to be found in line 360, in the middle of the second strophe: *Pantoporos aporos ep'ouden erchetai.* "Everywhere journeying, inexperienced and without issue, he comes to nothingness." The essential words are *pantoporos aporos.* The word *poros* means: passage through . . . , transition to . . . , path. Everywhere man makes himself a path; he ventures into all realms of the essent, of the overpowering power, and in so doing he is flung out of all paths. Herein is disclosed the entire strangeness of this strangest of all creatures: not only that he tries the essent in the whole of its strangeness, not only that in so doing he *is* a violent one striving beyond his familiar sphere. No, beyond all this he becomes the strangest of all beings because, without issue on all paths, he is cast out of every relation to the familiar and befallen by *atē*, ruin, catastrophe.

It is not hard to see that this *pantoporos aporos* contains an interpretation of *deinotaton*.

The interpretation is completed in the third salient phrase, line 370: *hypsipolis apolis*. In construction it is similar to *pantoporos aporos*, and its situation in the middle of the antistrophe presents another parallel. But it moves in a different direction. It speaks not of *poros* but of *polis;* not of the paths to all the realms of the essent but of the foundation and scene of man's being-there, the point at which all these paths meet, the *polis*. *Polis* is usually translated as city or city-state. This does not capture the full meaning. *Polis* means, rather, the place, the there, wherein and as which historical being-there is. The *polis* is the historical place, the there *in* which, *out of* which, and *for* which history happens. To this place and scene of history belong the gods, the temples, the priests, the festivals, the games, the poets, the thinkers, the ruler, the council of elders, the assembly of the people, the army and the fleet. All this does not first belong to the *polis*, does not become political by entering into a relation with a statesman and a general and the business of the state. No, it is political, i.e. at the site of history, provided there be (for example) poets *alone*, but then really poets, priests *alone*, but then really priests, rulers *alone*, but then really rulers. *Be*, but this means: as violent men to use power, to become pre-eminent in historical being as creators, as men of action. Pre-eminent in the historical place, they become at the same time *apolis*, without city and place, lonely, strange, and alien, without issue amid the essent as a whole, at the same time without statute and limit, without structure and order, because they themselves *as* creators must first create all this.

The first phase shows us the inner design of the essence of the strangest of all beings, the realms and scope of his power and his destiny. Now we go back to the beginning and attempt the second phase of interpretation.

The second phase. In the light of what has been said above we now follow the sequence of the strophes and hear how the being of man, the strangest of beings, unfolds. We shall try to determine when the *deinon* is meant in the first sense, how the *deinon* in the second sense emerges concurrently, and how, in the reciprocal relation between the two, the being of the strangest being is built up before us in its essential form.

The first strophe names the sea and the earth, each of them overpowering (*deinon*) in its way. It does not speak of them in the manner of us moderns who experience them as mere geographical and geological phenomena and then, as though by an afterthought, brush them over with a few faint and fleeting emotions. Here "sea" is said as though for the first time; the poet speaks of the wintry waves that the sea creates as it unceasingly tears open its own depths and unceasingly flings itself into them. Immediately after the main, guiding statement of the first verses, the song begins, hard and powerful, with *touto kai polion*. Man embarks on the groundless deep, forsaking the solid land. He sets sail not upon bright, smooth waters but amid the storms of winter. The account of this departure concerts with the movement of the prosody; the word *chōrei* in line 336 is situated at the point where the meter shifts: *chōrei*, he abandons the place, he starts out— and ventures into the preponderant power of the placeless waves. The word stands like a pillar in the edifice of these verses.

But woven into one with this violent excursion ⟨Aufbruch⟩ upon the overpowering sea is the never-resting incursion ⟨Einbruch⟩ into the indestructible power of the earth. Here the earth is the highest of the gods. Violently, with acts of power ⟨gewalt-tätig⟩ man disturbs the tranquillity of growth, the nurturing and maturing of the goddess who lives without effort. Here the overpowering reigns not in self-consuming wildness but without effort and fatigue; from out of the superior tranquillity of great riches, it produces and bestows the inexhaustible treasure that surpasses all zeal. Into this power bursts the violent one; year after year he breaks it open with his plows and drives the effortless earth into his restless endeavor. Sea and earth, departure and upheaval are joined by the *kai* in line 334, to which corresponds the *te* in line 338.

And now to all this the antistrophe: it names the birds in the air, the denizens of the water, bull and stallion in the mountains. The living things, lightly dreaming, living in their own rhythm and their own precinct, perpetually overflowing into new forms yet remaining in their *one* channel, know the place where they wander and pass the night. As living things, they are embedded in the power of the sea and the earth. Into this life as it rolls along self-contained, extraordinary in its own sphere and structure and ground, man casts his snares and nets; he snatches the living creatures out of their order, shuts them up in his pens and enclosures, and forces them under his yokes. On the one hand eruption and upheaval. On the other capture and constraint.

At this point, before we pass to the second strophe and its antistrophe, it is necessary to insert a note calculated to ward off a misinterpretation of the whole poem—a misinterpretation to which modern man readily inclines and which is indeed frequent. We have already pointed out that this is no description and exposition of the activities and fields of activity of man, an essent among other essents, but a poetic outline of his being, drawn from its extreme possibilities and limits. This in itself precludes the interpretation of this chorus as a narrative of man's development from the savage hunter and primitive sailor to the civilized builder of cities. Such a notion is the product of ethnology and psychological anthropology. It stems from the unwarranted application of a natural science—and a false one at that—to man's being. The basic fallacy underlying such modes of thought consists in the belief that history begins with the primitive and backward, the weak and helpless. The opposite is true. The beginning is the strangest and mightiest. What comes afterward is not development but the flattening that results from mere spreading out; it is inability to retain the beginning; the beginning is emasculated and exaggerated into a caricature of greatness taken as purely numerical and quantitative size and extension. That strangest of all beings *is* what he is *because* he harbors such a beginning in which everything all at once burst from superabundance into the overpowering and strove to master it.

If this beginning is inexplicable, it is not because of any deficiency in our knowledge of history. On the contrary, the authenticity and greatness of historical knowledge reside in an understanding of the mysterious character of this beginning. The knowledge of primordial history is not a ferreting out of primitive lore or a collecting of bones. It is neither half nor whole natural science but, if it is anything at all, mythology.

The first strophe and antistrophe speak of the sea, the earth, the animal, as the overpowering power which bursts into manifestness through the acts of the violent one.

Outwardly the second strophe passes from a description of the sea, the earth, animals to a characterization of man. But no more than the first strophe and antistrophe speak of nature in the restricted sense does the second strophe speak only of man.

No, what is now named—language, understanding, sentiment, passion, building—are no less a part of the overpowering power than sea, earth, and animal. The difference is only that the latter, the power that is man's environment, sustains, drives, inflames him, while the former reigns within him as the power which he, as the essent that he himself is, must take upon himself.

This pervading force becomes no less overpowering because man takes it into his power, which he uses as such. All this merely conceals the uncanniness of language, of the passions, the powers by which man is ordained ⟨gefügt⟩ as a historical being, while it seems to him that it is *he* who disposes ⟨verfügt⟩ of them. The strangeness, the uncanniness of these powers resides in their seeming familiarity. Directly they yield themselves to man only in their nonessence ⟨Unwesen⟩, so driving him and holding him out of his essence. In this way he comes to regard what is fundamentally more remote and overpowering than sea and earth as closest of all to him.

How far man is from being at home in his own essence is revealed by his opinion of himself as he who invented and could have invented language and understanding, building and poetry.

How could man ever have invented the power which pervades him, which alone enables him to *be* a man? We shall be wholly forgetting that this song speaks of the powerful (*deinon*), the strange and uncanny, if we suppose that the poet makes man invent such things as building and language. The word *edidaxato* does not mean: man invented, but: he found his way to the overpowering and therein first found himself: the violent one, the wielder of power. In view of what has been said, the "himself" means at once he who breaks out and breaks up ⟨ausbricht und umbricht, departs and plows⟩, he who captures and subjugates.

It is this breaking out and breaking up, capturing and subjugating that opens up the essent *as* sea, *as* earth, *as* animal. It happens only insofar as the powers of language, of understanding, of temperament, and of building are themselves mastered ⟨bewältigt⟩ in violence. The violence of poetic speech, of thinking projection, of building configuration, of the action that creates states is not a function of faculties that man has, but a taming and ordering of powers by virtue of which the essent opens up as such when man moves into it. This disclosure of the essent is the power that man must master in order to become himself amid the essent, i.e. in order to be historical. What is meant by *deinon* here in the second strophe must not be misinterpreted as invention or as a mere faculty or attribute of man.

Only if we understand that the use of power in language, in understanding, in forming and building helps to create (i.e. always, to bring forth) the violent act ⟨Gewalttat⟩ of laying out paths into the environing power of the essent, only then shall we understand the strangeness, the uncanniness of all violence. For man, as he journeys everywhere, is not without issue in the external sense that he comes up against outward barriers and cannot go on. In one way or another he can always go farther into the etcetera. He is without issue because he is always thrown back on the paths that he himself has laid out: he becomes mired in his paths, caught in the beaten track, and thus caught he compasses the circle of his world, entangles himself in appearance, and so excludes himself from being. He turns round and round in his own circle. He can ward off whatever threatens this limited sphere. He can employ every skill in its place. The violence that originally creates the paths engenders its own mischief of versatility, which is intrinsically issueless, so much so that it bars itself from reflection about the appearance in which it moves.

All violence shatters against *one* thing. That is death. It is an end beyond all consummation ⟨Vollendung⟩, a limit beyond all limits. Here there is no breaking-out or breaking-up, no capture or subjugation. But this strange and alien ⟨unheimlich⟩ thing that banishes us once and for all from everything in which we are at home is no particular event that must be named among others because it, too, ultimately happens. It is not only when he comes to die, but always and essentially that man is without issue in the face of death. Insofar as man *is,* he stands in the issuelessness of death. Thus his being-there is the happening of strangeness. (For us this happening of a strangeness must be initially grounded in human being-there.)

With the naming of *this* strange and powerful thing, the poetic project of being and human essence sets its own limit upon itself.

For the second antistrophe does not go on to name *still* other powers but gathers those already named into their inner unity. The concluding strophe carries the whole back to its basic line. But as we have stressed in the first phase, the basic line of what is actually at the center of the song (the *deinotaton*) resides precisely in the unitary relation between the two meanings of *deinon.* Accordingly the final strophe, in summary, names three things.

1. The power, the powerful, in which the action of the violent one moves, is the entire scope of the machination ⟨Machenschaft⟩, *machanoen,* entrusted to him. We do not take the word "machination" in a disparaging sense. We have in mind something essential that is disclosed to us in the Greek word *technē. Technē* means neither art nor skill, to say nothing of technique in the modern sense. We translate *technē* by "knowledge." But this requires explanation. Knowledge means here not the result of mere observations concerning previously unknown data. Such information, though indispensable for knowledge, is never more than accessory. Knowledge in the authentic sense of *technē* is the initial and persistent looking out beyond what is given at any time. In different ways, by different channels, and in different realms, this transcendence ⟨Hinaussein⟩ effects ⟨setzt ins Werk⟩ what

first gives the datum its relative justification, its potential determinateness, and hence its limit. Knowledge is the ability to
put into work the being of any particular essent. The Greeks
called art in the true sense and the work of art *technē*, because art is what most immediately brings being (i.e. the appearing that stands there in itself) to stand, stabilizes it in
something present (the work). The work of art is a work not
primarily because it is wrought ⟨ gewirkt ⟩, made, but because
it brings about ⟨ er-wirkt ⟩ being in an essent; it brings about
the phenomenon in which the emerging power, *physis*, comes
to shine ⟨ scheinen ⟩. It is through the work of art as essent being that everything else that appears and is to be found is first
confirmed and made accessible, explicable, and understand-
able as being or not being.

Because art in a pre-eminent sense stabilizes and manifests
being in the work as an essent, it may be regarded as the
ability, pure and simple, to accomplish, to put-into-the-work
⟨ ins-Werk-setzen ⟩, as *technē*. This accomplishment is a manifesting realization ⟨ Erwirken ⟩ of being *in* the essent. This superior, realizing opening and keeping open is knowledge. The
passion of knowledge is inquiry. Art is knowledge and therefore *technē*. Art is not *technē* because it involves "technical"
skill, tools, materials.

Thus *technē* provides the basic trait of *deinon*, the violent;
for violence ⟨ Gewalt-tätigkeit ⟩ is the use of power ⟨ Gewalt-
brauchen ⟩ against the overpowering ⟨ Überwältigende ⟩:
through knowledge it wrests being from concealment into the
manifest as the essent.

2. Just as *deinon* as violence collects its essence in the fundamental Greek word *technē*, so *deinon* as the overpowering
is manifested in the equally fundamental *dikēo*. We translate
it as Fug.* Here we understand Fug first in the sense of joint
and framework ⟨ Fuge und Gefüge ⟩; then as decree, dispen-
sation, a directive that the overpowering imposes on its reign;
finally, as the governing structure ⟨ das fügende Gefüge ⟩

---

* Heidegger is particularly free to define the word "Fug" as he
wishes because the word does not occur in modern literary German
except in the combination "mit Fug und Recht"—"with F. and
justice," where it conveys no precise meaning but suggests "proper
order," "fitness." This is why I have preferred to introduce the word
in German. R.M.

which compels adaptation ⟨Einfügung⟩ and compliance ⟨Sichfügen⟩.

If *dikē* is translated as "justice" taken in a juridical, moral sense, the word loses its fundamental metaphysical meaning. The same applies to the interpretation of *dikē* as norm. In all its realms and dominions the overpowering, in respect to its domination, is Fug. Being, *physis*, as power, is basic and original togetherness: *logos;* it is governing order ⟨fügender Fug⟩: *dikē.*

Thus the *deinon* as the overpowering (*dikē*) and the *deinon* as the violent (*technē*) confront one another, though not as two given things. In this confrontation *technē* bursts forth against *dikē*, which in turn, as Fug, the commanding order, disposes ⟨verfügt⟩ of all *technē*. The reciprocal confrontation *is*. It is only insofar as the strangest thing of all, being-human, is actualized, insofar as man is present as history.

3. The basic trait of the *deinotaton* lies in the interrelation between the two meanings of *deinon*. The sapient man sails into the very middle of the dominant order ⟨Fug⟩; he tears it open and violently carries being into the essent; yet he can never master the overpowering. Hence he is tossed back and forth between structure and the structureless, order and mischief ⟨Fug and Un-fug⟩, between the evil and the noble. Every violent curbing of the powerful is either victory or defeat. Both, each in its different way, fling him out of home, and thus, each in its different way, unfold the dangerousness of achieved or lost being. Both, in different ways, are menaced by disaster. The *violent one,* the creative man, who sets forth into the un-said, who breaks into the un-thought, compels the unhappened to happen and makes the unseen appear —this violent one stands at all times in venture (*tolma,* line 371). In venturing to master being, he must risk the assault of the nonessent, *mē kalon,* he must risk dispersion, in-stability, disorder, mischief. The higher the summit of historical being—there, the deeper will be the abyss, the more abrupt the fall into the unhistorical, which merely thrashes around in issue-less and placeless confusion.

Arrived at the end of the second phase, we may wonder what purpose can be served by a third.

The third phase. The central truth of the song was set forth in the first phase. The second phase has led us through all the essential realms of the powerful and violent. The final strophe pulls the whole together into the essence of him who is strangest of all. Certain details might be considered and elucidated more fully. But this would provide a mere appendage to what has already been said; it would not necessitate a new phase of interpretation. If we content ourselves with what the poem directly says, the interpretation is at an end. Actually it has just begun. The actual interpretation must show what does not stand in the words and is nevertheless said. To accomplish this the exegete must use violence. He must seek the essential where nothing more is to be found by the scientific interpretation that brands as unscientific everything that transcends its limits.

But here, where we must restrict ourselves to a single poem, we can undertake this third phase only from a limited point of view imposed by our main task, and even here we must confine ourselves to a few steps. Bearing in mind what has been said in the first phase, we start from the results of our explanation of the final strophe in the second phase.

The *deinotaton* of the *deinon*, the strangest of the strange, lies in the conflict between *dikē* and *technē*. The strangest is not the extreme rectilinear intensification of the strange. It is specifically the uniquely strange. The conflict between the overwhelming presence of the essent as a whole and man's violent being-there creates the possibility of downfall into the issueless and placeless: disaster. But disaster and the possibility of disaster do not occur only at the end, when a single act of power fails, when the violent one makes a false move; no, this disaster is fundamental, it governs and waits in the conflict between violence and the overpowering. Violence against the preponderant power of being *must* shatter against being, if being rules in its essence, as *physis*, as emerging power.

But this necessity of disaster can only subsist insofar as what must shatter is driven into such a being-there. Man is forced into such a being-there, hurled into the affliction ⟨Not⟩* of such being, because the overpowering as such, in

---

* The dictionary meanings of the German word "Not" are need, want, anguish, distress, affliction, peril, necessity. Insofar as one meaning can be disengaged from the whole, Heidegger's primary

order to appear in its power, *requires* a place, a scene of disclosure. The essence of being-human opens up to us only when understood through this need compelled by being itself. The being-there of historical man means: to be posited as the breach into which the preponderant power of being bursts in its appearing, in order that this breach itself should shatter against being.

The strangest (man) is what it is because, fundamentally, it cultivates and guards the familiar, only in order to break out of it and to let what overpowers it break in. Being itself hurls man into this breaking-away, which drives him beyond himself to venture forth toward being, to accomplish being, to stabilize it in the work, and so hold open the essent as a whole. Therefore the violent one knows no kindness and conciliation ⟨ Güte und Begütigung ⟩ (in the usual sense); he cannot be mollified or appeased by success or prestige. In all this the violent, creative man sees only the semblance of fulfillment, and this he despises. In willing the unprecedented, he casts aside all help. To him disaster is the deepest and broadest affirmation of the overpowering. In the shattering of the wrought work, in the knowledge that it is mischief ⟨ Unfug ⟩ and *sarma* (a dunghill), he leaves the overpowering to its order ⟨ Fug ⟩. But all this not in the form of "psychic experiences" in which the soul of the creative man wallows, and still less in the form of petty feelings of inferiority, but wholly in terms of the accomplishment itself, the putting-into-the work. *As history* the overpowering, being, is confirmed in works.

Thus the being-there of the historical man is the breach through which the being embodied in the essent can open. As such it is an *in-cident* ⟨ Zwischen-fall, a fall-between ⟩, the incident in which suddenly the unbound powers of being come forth and are accomplished as history. The Greeks had a profound sense of this suddenness and uniqueness of being-there, forced on them by being itself, which disclosed itself

---

meaning is "need," because he has used this word "Not" as a translation for *chre* in the sixth fragment of Parmenides. But the word as used in German speech and poetry carries the primary implication of distress, trouble, affliction.

to them as *physis* and *logos* and *dikē*. It is inconceivable that the Greeks should have decided to turn out culture for the benefit of the next few millennia of Western history. In the unique need of their being-there they alone responded solely with violence, thus not doing away with the need but only augmenting it; and in this way they won for themselves the fundamental condition of true historical greatness.

We shall fail to understand the mysteriousness of the essence of being-human, thus experienced and poetically carried back to its ground, if we snatch at value judgments of any kind.

The evaluation of being-human as arrogance and presumption in the pejorative sense takes man out of his essential need as the in-cident. To judge in this way is to take man as something already-there, to put this something into an empty space, and appraise it according to some external table of values. But it is the same kind of misunderstanding to interpret the poet's words as a tacit rejection of being-human, a covert admonition to resign oneself without violence, to seek undisturbed comfort. This interpretation might even find some basis in the concluding lines of the poem.

One who is *thus* (namely the strangest of all) should be excluded from hearth and council. But the final words of the chorus do not contradict what has previously been said about being-human. Insofar as the chorus turns *against* the strangest of all, it says that this manner of being is *not* that of every day. Such being-there is not to be found in the usual bustle and activity. There is nothing surprising about these concluding words; indeed, we should have to be surprised if they were lacking. Their attitude of rejection is a direct and complete confirmation of the strangeness and uncanniness of human being. With its concluding words the song swings back to its beginning.

But what has all this to do with Parmenides' maxim? The maxim speaks nowhere of strangeness. Almost too coolly it limits itself to the belonging-together of apprehension and being. In considering the meaning of this bond we have digressed into an interpretation of Sophocles. How does this interpretation help us? Can we simply transpose it into an

interpretation of Parmenides? No, we cannot. But we must
remind ourselves of the essential and initial connection between poetic and philosophical discourse; particularly when,
as here, we are dealing with the poetry and thinking that first
awakened and established the historical being-there of a people. But beyond this general relation, we find a definite trait
of meaning that is common both to the poem and the philosophical maxim.

In our second phase, in summing up the final strophe, we
advisedly stressed the reciprocal relation between *dikē* and
technē. *Technē* is the overpowering order. *Dikē* is the violence of knowledge. The reciprocal relation between them is
the happening of strangeness.

We now maintain that the bond between *noein* (apprehension) and *einai* (being) stated in the maxim of Parmenides
is nothing other than this relation. If this is confirmed, we
have proved our former contention that this maxim for the
first time delimits the essence of being-human and does not
just happen to speak of man in some indifferent respect.

In proof of our assertion we shall first work out two general
considerations. Then we shall attempt a detailed exegesis of
the maxim.

In the poetic relation between *dikē* and *technē*, *dikē* stands
for the being of the essent as a whole. Even earlier than Sophocles we encounter this use of the word among the Greeks. The
oldest saying that has come down to us, that of Anaximander,
speaks of being in an essential connection with *dikē*.

Similarly Heraclitus speaks of *dikē* in making an essential
statement about being. Fragment 80 begins: *eidenai de chrē
ton polemon eonta xynon kai dikē erin.* "It is necessary to bear
in mind setting-apart ⟨Aus-einander-Setzung⟩ as essentially
bringing-together and order ⟨Fug⟩ as contending . . ." *Dikē*
as the governing structure belongs to contending setting-apart.
This contending setting-apart is also *physis*, which in emerging, causes the appearing to shine (to be present), and accordingly it is being (cf. Fragments 23 and 28).

Finally, Parmenides himself is a crucial witness to the philosophical use of the word *dikē* in speaking of being. For him
Dikē is a goddess. She guards the alternately closing and opening keys to the gates of day and night, i.e. to the paths of be-

ing (that discloses), of appearance (that distorts) and nothingness (that closes). This means that the essent discloses
itself only insofar as the structure ⟨Fug⟩ of being is guarded
and preserved. Being as *dikē* is the key to the essent in its
structure. This meaning of *dikē* follows beyond a doubt from
the thirty mighty opening verses of Parmenides' didactic poem
that have come down to us. It becomes clear that both the
poetic and the philosophical discourse on being name, i.e.
create and define, it with the same word, *dikē*.

The other general consideration necessary for the proof of
our assertion is this. It has already been pointed out how in
apprehension ⟨Vernehmung⟩ as ac-cepting anticipation ⟨Vor-
nehmung⟩ the essent as such is disclosed and so comes forth
from concealment. For the poet, the assault of *technē* against
dikē is the happening whereby man ceases to be at home. In
his exile from home, the home is first disclosed as such. But
in one with it and only thus, the alien, the overpowering, is
disclosed as such. Through the event of homelessness the
whole of the essent is disclosed. In this disclosure unconcealment takes place. But this is nothing other than the happening of the unfamiliar.

Yes, to be sure, one might answer, that is true of what the
poet says. But what we miss in the sober maxim of Parmenides
is the strangeness of which we have been speaking.

Accordingly it is incumbent upon us to show this sober
thought in its true light. This we shall do by a detailed interpretation. In advance we say: if it should turn out that apprehension ⟨Vernehmung⟩ in its bond with being (*dikē*)
demands violence and as violence is a need ⟨Not⟩ endured
only in struggle in the sense of *polemos* and *eris;* if in the
course of this demonstration it further turns out that apprehension is expressly related to the logos and that this logos
proves to be the ground of being-human, then our assertion
of the inner kinship between the philosophical maxim and
the poem will have been confirmed.

We shall show three things:

1. Apprehension is no mere process, but a de-cision.
2. Apprehension stands in an essential kinship with the
logos. The logos is a need.
3. The logos is the essential foundation of language. As

such it is a struggle and the ground on which man's historical being-there is built in the midst of the essent as a whole.

Ad 1. To grasp adequately the essence of *noein,* apprehension, it does not suffice to avoid lumping it together with the activity of thought or with judgments. We have characterized apprehension above as a receptive attitude toward the appearing of the essent. As such it is an independent departure upon a distinct path. But this implies that apprehension cuts across the intersection of the three paths. This it can do only if it is through and through a decision *for* being *against* nothing and thus a struggle *with* appearance. But such essential decision must use violence if it is to persevere against the continuous pressure of involvement in the everyday and commonplace. The violence of this decisive departure along the path to the being of the essent wrests man out of his home in what happens to be nearest and most familiar to him.

Only if we understand apprehension as such a departure shall we be fortified against the fallacy that consists in interpreting it as just another of man's activities, as a self-explanatory use of his spiritual faculties or even some psychological process that just happens to go on. No, apprehension is wrested from the habitual press of living—and by a contrary movement. Its bond with the being of the essent does not make itself. To name it is not merely to ascertain a fact, but points to the struggle by which it is forged. The maxim is sober in the manner of philosophy for which the basic form of pathos is the strictness of conceptual thought.

Ad 2. We have cited Fragment 6 by way of explaining the differentiation of the three paths. In so doing we purposely postponed a detailed interpretation of the first verse. Meanwhile we have come to read and hear it differently: *Chrē to legein te noein t'eon emmenai.* But even then we translated: "Needful is the gathered* setting-forth as well as the apprehension of this: the essent (is) being." We have seen that here *noein* and *legein,* apprehension and logos, are mentioned together, and also that *chrē* is set emphatically at the begin-

---

* Heidegger misquotes himself slightly. See the translation above, p. 94. There "sammelnd" (gathering), here "gesammelt" (gathered), there "Seiend in dessen Sein," here "das Seiend (ist) Sein." "von diesem" is added. R.M.

ning of the verse. Needful are apprehension and logos. *Legein* is mentioned along with *apprehension* as a process of the same character. Indeed, *legein* is mentioned first. Logos here cannot mean ingathering as the hinge of being, but must, equated with apprehension, signify the (human) act of violence, by which being is gathered in its togetherness. Needful is collection as it pertains to apprehension. Both must happen "for the sake of being." Ingathering means here: to collect oneself amid dispersion into the impermanent, to recapture oneself out of confusion in appearance. But this gathering that is still a turning-away can be accomplished only through the gathering which is a turning-to, which draws the essent into the togetherness of being. Thus logos as ingathering becomes a need ⟨Not⟩ and parts from logos in the sense of the to-getherness of being (*physis*). It is *logos* as ingathering, as man's collecting-himself toward fitness ⟨Fug⟩, that first brings being-human into its essence, so thrusting it into homelessness, insofar as the home is dominated by the appearance of the ordinary, customary, and commonplace.

It remains to be asked why the *legein* is mentioned before the *noein*. The answer is: it is from the *legein* that the *noein* first takes its essence as gathering apprehension.

This definition of the essence of being-human at the beginning of Western philosophy is not accomplished by seizing upon any attributes in the living creature called "man" as opposed to other living creatures. Being-human defines itself from out of a relation to what is as a whole. The human *essence* shows itself here to be the relation which first opens up being to man. Being-human, as the need ⟨Not⟩ of apprehension and collection, is a being-driven ⟨Nötigung⟩ into the freedom of undertaking *technē*, the sapient embodiment of being. This is the character of history.

From the essence of *logos* as gathering there follows an essential consequence for the character of the *legein*. Because *legein* as gathering thus defined is related to the original to-getherness of being, and because being means to come into unconcealment, this gathering has a fundamental character of opening, making manifest. *Legein* thus enters into a clear and sharp opposition to concealing and hiding.

This is directly and unmistakably attested by a maxim of

Heraclitus. Fragment 93 says: "The ruler whose prophesy occurs at Delphi *oute legei oute kryptei,* neither gathers nor hides, *alla sēmainei,* but gives hints." Here gathering stands in opposition to hiding. To gather is here to disclose, to make manifest.

Here I think we may ask the simple question: whence can the word *legein,* to collect, have obtained the meaning to make manifest (un-conceal) in opposition to conceal, if not on the strength of its essential relation to *logos* in the sense of *physis?* The power which emerging shows itself is unconcealment. Accordingly *legein* means: to produce the unconcealed as such, to produce the essent in its unconcealment. Thus the *logos,* not only in Heraclitus but still in Plato, has the character of *dēloun,* making manifest. Aristotle characterizes the *legein* of the *logos* as *apophainesthai,* to bring-to-show-itself (see *Sein und Zeit* §§ 7 and 44). Since the vitiation of the meaning of *logos* that was to make logic possible set in precisely with Plato and Aristotle, this characterization of *legein* as to disclose and make manifest strongly indicates that this was the original meaning. Ever since then, for two thousand years, these ties between *logos, alētheia, physis, noein,* and *idea* have remained hidden in unintelligibility.

But in the beginning: *logos* as the gathering that makes manifest, and in the same sense being as fitness ⟨Fug⟩ or *physis,* became the necessary essence of historical man. Thence it takes only a step to understand how *logos,* thus understood, determined the essence of language and how *logos* became a name for discourse. In accordance with its historical, history-disclosing essence, being-human is *logos,* the gathering and apprehending of the being of the essent: it is the happening of that strangest essent of all, in whom through violence, through acts of power ⟨Gewalt-tätigkeit⟩, the overpowering is made manifest and made to stand. But the chorus from *Antigone* has told us: simultaneously with man's departure into being he finds himself in the word, in language.

In connection with the question of the essence of language, the question of its origin has arisen time and time again. Men have sought the answer in remote ways. And there lies the first, crucial answer to the question: The origin of language remains a mystery; not because men have not been clever

enough, but because their sharpness and cleverness made a
false move before even setting to work. The origin of language is in essence mysterious. And this means that language
can only have arisen from the overpowering, the strange and
terrible, through man's departure into being. In this departure
language was being, embodied in the word: poetry. Language
is the primordial poetry in which a people speaks being. Conversely, the great poetry by which a people enters into history
initiates the molding of its language. The Greeks created and
experienced this poetry through Homer. Language was manifested to their being-there as departure into being, as a configuration disclosing the essent.

It is by no means self-evident that language is logos, collection. But we understand this interpretation of language as
logos when we consider the beginning of the historical being-
there of the Greeks, the basic direction in which being disclosed itself to them and in which they brought it to stand,
stabilized it, in the essent.

The word, the name, restores the emerging essent from the
immediate, overpowering surge to its being and maintains it
in this openness, delimitation, and permanence. Naming does
not come afterward, providing an already manifest essent with
a designation and a hallmark known as a word; it is the other
way around: originally an act of violence that discloses being,
the word sinks from this height to become a mere sign, and
this sign proceeds to thrust itself before the essent. Pristine
speech opens up the being of the essent in the structure of its
collectedness. And this opening is collected in a second sense:
the word preserves what was originally collected and so ad-
ministers ⟨ verwaltet ⟩ the overpowering power. Standing and
active in logos, which is ingathering, man is the gatherer. He
undertakes to govern and succeeds in governing the power of
the overpowering.

But we know that this violence is the strangest, the uncan-
niest thing of all. Impelled by *tolma*, daring, man comes necessarily to evil as well as to the brave and noble. Where
language speaks as violent gathering, as a curbing of the
overpowering, and as a safeguarding, then and then alone
will there necessarily be a breaking of bonds ⟨ Ungebunden-
heit ⟩ and loss. Consequently language, speech, is at the same

time idle talk, a concealment rather than disclosure of being, dispersion, disorder and mischief ⟨ Unfug ⟩ rather than a gathering into structure and order. All by itself the logos does not make language. The *legein* is a *need: chrē to legein*, needful is the gathering apprehension of the being of the essent. (Why this need?)

Ad 3. Because the essence of language is found in the act of gathering within the togetherness of being, language as everyday speech comes to its truth only when speaking and hearing are oriented toward logos as collectedness in the sense of being. For in being and its structure, the essent is originally and crucially, in advance as it were, a *legomenon*, collected, said, pro-nounced ⟨ vor- und hervorgesprochen ⟩. Now at last we understand the full context of Parmenides' saying that *"noein"* ⟨ apprehension ⟩ happens for the sake of being.

The passage runs (Fragment 8, lines 34–6): "There is an inherent bond between apprehension and that for the sake of which apprehension occurs.* For not without the essent in which it (being) is already spoken, will you find (attain) apprehension." Its relation to the logos as *physis* makes *legein* into an apprehending gathering, and makes apprehension a gatherer. Therefore the *legein*, if it is to remain collected, must turn away from all mere hearsay, all mouthing and glibness. And indeed Parmenides himself makes a sharp contrast between *logos* and *glōssa* (Fragment 7, lines 3 ff.). The passage corresponds to the beginning of Fragment 6, which, referring to the first, indispensable path to being, says that it is needful to collect oneself, to concentrate, on the being of the essent. Here ⟨ in Fragment 7 ⟩ Parmenides gives counsel for the traveling of the third path, the path into appearance. It leads through the essent which also stands in semblance. It is the customary path. Therefore the sapient man must unremittingly put himself back from this path into the *legein* and *noein* of the being of the essent:

and let not cunning habit drive you toward this path,
making you lose yourself in sightless gaping and noisy hearing
and glibness; instead discriminate and decide ⟨ entscheide
    scheidend ⟩,

* This quotation is translated somewhat differently on p. 117.
R.M.

setting before you, gathered in one, the counsel of multiple
    conflict,
given by me.

Logos here stands in the closest connection with *krinein*,
to separate ⟨ Scheiden ⟩ in the sense of de-cide ⟨ Entscheiden ⟩
in collecting toward the collectedness of being. Selection ⟨ das
auslesende "Lesen" ⟩ is the foundation and proof of the pur-
suit of being and the battle against appearance. The meaning
of *krinein* includes to pick out, to favor, to set a measure that
will determine rank.

These three points carry our interpretation of the fragment
far enough to show that Parmenides too speaks in essential
respects of logos. Logos is a need ⟨ Not ⟩ and intrinsically requires violence to ward off mouthing and dispersion. Logos
as *legein* opposes *physis*. In this decision logos as gathering
becomes the ground of being-human. That is why we were able
to say that the decisive definition of man's essence was accomplished for the very first time in this saying. To be a man
means to *take* gathering *upon oneself*, to undertake a gathering apprehension of the being of the essent, the sapient in-
corporation of appearing in the work, and so to *administer*
⟨ verwalten ⟩ unconcealment, to *preserve* it against cloaking
and concealment.

Thus at the very beginning of Western philosophy it became evident that the question of being necessarily embraces
the foundations of being-there.

This connection between being and being-there (and the
corresponding inquiry into it) is not so much as touched by
epistemological formulations of the question, and still less by
the superficial observation that every view of being is dependent on a view of man. (An inquiry into being that is
concerned not only with the being of the essent but with
being itself in *its* essence calls explicitly for a grounding of
being-there in the question of being. For this reason and *only*
for this reason we have given this grounding the name of
"*fundamental* ontology." See *Sein und Zeit*, Introduction.)

We say that this initial disclosure of the essence of being-
human was *decisive*. But it was not preserved and held fast
as the great beginning. It had an entirely different conse-

quence: the definition—which later gained currency in the West and which remains unshaken in the dominant opinion and attitude—of man as the rational animal. By way of demonstrating the gulf between this definition and the initial disclosure of man's essence, we select formulae embodying the beginning and the end. The end discloses itself in the formula *anthrōpos = zōion logon echon:* man, the animal equipped with reason. For the beginning we improvise a formula which at the same time sums up our reflections up to this point: *physis = logos anthrōpon echōn:* being, overpowering appearing, necessitates the gathering which pervades and grounds being-human.

The end, to be sure, retains a vestige of the connection between logos and being-human, but the logos has long since been externalized into a faculty of understanding and reason. The faculty itself is based on the existence ⟨ Vorhandensein ⟩ of animals of a special kind, on the *zōion beltiston,* the animal that has turned out best (Xenophon).

Quite on the contrary, being-human was initially grounded in the disclosure of the being of the essent.

In the perspective of the common and prevailing definitions; in the perspective of modern and contemporary metaphysics, theory of knowledge, anthropology, and ethics, all determined by Christianity, our interpretation of the fragment must appear to be an arbitrary distortion. We are accused of reading into it things that an "exact interpretation" can never determine. This is true. In the usual present-day view what has been said here is a mere product of the farfetched and one-sided Heideggerian method of exegesis, which has already become proverbial. But here we may, indeed, we must ask: Which interpretation is the true one, the one which simply takes over a perspective into which it has fallen, because this perspective, this line of sight, presents itself as familiar and self-evident; or the interpretation which questions the customary perspective from top to bottom, because conceivably—and indeed actually—this line of sight does not lead to what is in need of being seen.

True—to give up the familiar and go back to an interpretation that is also a questioning is a jump. In order to jump one has to take a proper run. It is the run that decides everything;

for it implies that we ourselves really *ask* the questions and in these questions first create our perspectives. But this is not done shiftily and arbitrarily, nor is it done by clinging to a system set up as a norm, but in and out of historical necessity ⟨Notwendigkeit⟩, out of the need ⟨Not⟩ of historical being-there.

Legein and *noein,* to gather and to apprehend, are a need and an act of violence *against* the overpowering, but at the same time only and always *for* it. Time and time again the violent ones must shrink back in fear from this use of force and yet they are unable to forego it. Amid this reluctant will to mastery, the suspicion is bound to flare up at times that perhaps the overpowering will be most securely and completely dominated if the concealment of being—the emerging power, whose essence is *logos,* the collectedness of the conflicting—is simply preserved, if in a certain sense every possibility of appearing, of manifestation, is denied. The violence of the strangest of all beings comprises this presumption (which actually implies the highest recognition): to overpower the appearing power by declining all openness toward it, to withstand it by denying its omnipotence the site in which to manifest itself.

But for being-there such refusal of openness toward being means to renounce its essence, which demands: emerge from being or never enter into being-there. And this is expressed by Sophocles in a chorus from the tragedy of *Oedipus in Colonus,* lines 1224 f.: *mē phynai ton hapanta ni/kāi logon,* "never to have entered into being-there prevails over the togetherness of the essent as a whole."

Never to have taken being-there upon oneself, *mē phynai,* is said of man, of man who as the gatherer of *physis* is essentially gathered *with* it. Here *physis, phynai* are used in regard to man's being, while *logos* is used in the Heraclitean sense, as the reigning order of the essent as a whole. These poetic words express the intimate relation of being-there to being and its disclosure; they do so by naming what is remotest from being, namely not-being-there. Here the strangest and most terrible possibility of being-there is revealed: the possibility of breaking the preponderant power of being by a supreme act of violence against itself. Being-there has this possibility not as an empty evasion; no, insofar as it is, being-there *is* this possibility, for as being-there it must, in every act of violence, shatter against being.

This looks like pessimism. But it would be wrong to apply this term to Greek being-there. Not because the Greeks were basically optimistic but because these terms have no relevance to Greek life. The Greeks were more pessimistic than a pessimist can ever be. But they were also more optimistic than any optimist. Their historical being-there preceded optimism and pessimism.

To speak of optimism or pessimism is to look on being-there as a business proposition, successful or unsuccessful. This attitude is expressed in Schopenhauer's well-known words: "Life is a business that doesn't cover its costs." What makes this proposition untrue is not that "life" does cover its costs in the end, but that life (as being-there) is simply not a business. True, for the last few centuries it has become one. And that is why Greek being-there is so mysterious to us.

Not-being-there is the supreme victory over being. Being-there is unremitting affliction resulting from defeat and renewed attempts at violence against being: at the site of its appearing, omnipotent being (literally) violates ⟨vergewaltigt, to do violence to, to rape⟩ being-there; being indeed is this site, surrounding and controlling ⟨umwaltet und durchwaltet⟩ being-there and so holding it in being.

Logos and *physis* move apart, but *logos* does not yet break away from *physis*. That is to say, it does not yet confront the being of the essent in such a way, it does not yet take such an attitude "toward" it, as to appoint itself (as reason) a court of justice over being; it does not yet undertake the task of determining and regulating the being of the essent.

This development sets in only when the logos loses its initial essence, when being as *physis* is veiled and misinterpreted. Man's being-there changes accordingly. The slow end of this history, the slow end in which we have long been standing, is the domination of thinking as *ratio* (in the sense of understanding as well as reason) over the *being* of the essent. Here begins the contest between "rationalism and irrationalism" that has been in progress to this day in every conceivable disguise and under the most contradictory titles. Irrationalism is only the obvious weakness and failure of rationalism and hence itself a kind of rationalism. Irrationalism is a way out of rationalism, an escape which does not lead into the open but merely entangles us more in rationalism, because it gives rise to the opinion that we can overcome rationalism by merely saying no to it, whereas this only makes its machinations the more dangerous by hiding them from view.

In this lecture we do not propose to describe the interior history of this domination of thought (as the *ratio* of logic) over the being of the essent. Aside from the inherent difficulty of such an undertaking, such an account can have no historical cogency until we ourselves have awakened the energies of independent questioning from out of, and for the sake of, our own history in its present hour.

Nevertheless it is necessary to show how the initial separation between *logos* and *physis* led to the secession of the logos, which became the starting point for the domination of reason.

This secession of the logos which started logos on its way to becoming a court of justice over being occurred in Greek philosophy itself. Indeed, it brought about the end of Greek philosophy. We shall only master Greek philosophy as the beginning of Western philosophy if we also understand this beginning in the beginning of its end. For the ensuing period it was only this end that became the "beginning," so much so that it concealed the original beginning. But this beginning of the end of the great beginning, the philosophy of Plato and Aristotle, remains great even if we totally discount the greatness of its Western consequences.

Now we asked: How did this secession of the logos, this priority of logos over being, come about? How did the separation between being and thinking enter upon its decisive form? Here we can only sketch this history in a few bold strokes. We start from the end and ask:

1. What was the relation between *physis* and *logos* at the end of Greek philosophy, in Plato and Aristotle? How was *physis* understood? What form and function had *logos* assumed?

2. How did this end come about? What was the actual ground of the transformation?

Ad 1. In the end the word *idea, eidon,* "idea," came to the fore as the decisive and predominant name for being (*physis*). Since then the interpretation of being as idea has dominated all Western thinking throughout the history of its transformations down to the present day. This origin also explains why, in the great and definitive culmination of the first period of Western thinking, in the system of Hegel, the reality of the real, being in the absolute sense, is conceived as "idea" and expressly so called. But what does it mean that *physis* should have been interpreted as *idea* in Plato?

In our first introductory characterization of the Greek experience of being, we listed *idea, eidos* among other names for it. In reading the philosophy of Hegel or of any other modern thinker, or in studying medieval Scholasticism, we frequently run across the use of the word "idea" for *being*. This, if we are not mistaken, is *incomprehensible* on the basis of current ideas. But we understand it readily if we start from the beginning of Greek philosophy. Then we can instantly measure the distance between the interpretations of being as *physis* and as *idea*.

The word *idea* means that which is seen in the visible, the aspect it offers. What is offered is the appearance, *eidos*, of what confronts us. The appearance of a thing is that wherein, as we say, it presents, introduces itself to us, places itself before ⟨ vor-stellt ⟩ us and as such stands before us, that wherein and as such it is present, i.e. in the Greek sense, *is*. This standing is the stability of that which has emerged from out of itself, of *physis*. But from the standpoint of man this standing-there of the stable and permanent is at the same time the surface of what is present *through itself*, the apprehensible. In the appearance, the present, the essent, presents its what and how. It is apprehended and taken, it is in the possession of an acceptance, its property ⟨ Habe ⟩, it is the accessible presence of the present: *ousia*. Thus *ousia* can signify both: the presence of something present *and* this present thing in the what of its appearance ⟨ Aussehen ⟩.

Herein is concealed the source of the subsequent distinction between *existentia* and *essentia*. (Whereas if we blindly take over the traditional and current differentiation of *existentia* and *essentia*, we shall never understand how precisely *existentia* and *essentia* and the difference between them stand out from the being of the essent and thereby characterize it.

But if we understand *idea* (appearance) as presence, it reveals itself in a twofold sense as Ständigkeit ⟨ stability, standingness ⟩. In the appearance there lies first the standing-out-of-unconcealment, the simple *estin*. In the appearance is disclosed second that which appears, that *which* stands, the *ti estin*.⟩

Thus the *idea* constitutes the essent. But here *idea* and *eidos* are used in an extended sense, not only for that which is visible to the physical eye but for everything that can be perceived. *What* an essent is lies in its appearance, but the appearance presents (makes *present*) the what.

But, we shall have asked by now, is this interpretation of being as *idea* not genuinely Greek? After all, it arises with undeniable necessity from the experience of being as *physis,* as emerging power, as appearing, as standing-in-the-light. What does that which appears show in its appearing ⟨ Erscheinen ⟩ if not its appearance ⟨ Aussehen ⟩, the *idea?* In what way does the interpretation of being as *idea* differ from the interpretation as *physis?* Is the tradition not perfectly right in seeing Greek philosophy—as it has done for centuries—in the light of Platonic philosophy? Far from representing an opposition to the beginning, not to say a decline, Plato's interpretation of being actually develops and sharpens this beginning and grounds it in the "theory of ideas." Plato is the completion of the beginning.

Actually it cannot be denied that the interpretation of being as *idea* results from the basic experience of being as *physis.* It is, as we say, a necessary consequence of the essence of being as emerging Scheinen ⟨ seeming, appearing, radiance ⟩. And herein there is no departure, not to mention a falling-off, from the beginning. No, that is true.

But if the essential *consequence* is exalted to the level of the essence itself and takes the place of the essence, what then? Then we have a falling-off, which must in turn produce strange consequences. And that is what happened. The crux of the matter is not that *physis* should have been characterized as *idea* but that the *idea* should have become the sole and decisive interpretation of being.

We can easily appraise the distance between the two interpretations if we consider the difference between the perspectives in which these two definitions of being, *physis* and *idea*, move. *Physis* is the emerging power, the standing-there-in-itself, stability. *Idea*, appearance as what is seen, is a determination of the stable insofar and only insofar as it encounters vision. But *physis* as emerging power is by the same token an appearing. Except that the appearing is ambiguous. Appearing means first: that which gathers itself, which brings-itself-to-stand in its togetherness and so stands. But second it means: that which, already standing-there, presents a front, a surface, offers an appearance to be looked at.

From the standpoint of space, the difference between appearing and appearing is this: appearing in the first and authentic sense as bringing-itself-to-stand in togetherness involves space, which it first conquers; as it stands there, it creates space for itself; it produces space and everything pertaining to it; it is not copied. Appearing in the second sense emerges from an already finished space; it is situated in the rigid measures of this space, and we see it by looking toward it. The vision makes the thing. Now this vision becomes decisive, instead of the thing itself. Appearing in the first sense opens up space. Appearing in the second sense merely circumscribes and measures the space that has already been opened.

But does not Parmenides' maxim say: Being and apprehension—that which is seen and the act of seeing—belong together? Yes, to be sure, the thing seen belongs to seeing, but from this it does not follow that being-seen alone determines, or could determine, the presence of the thing seen. Parmenides' maxim does not say that being should be understood on the basis of apprehension, i.e. as something merely apprehended; it says rather that apprehension should be considered for the sake of being. Apprehension should so disclose the essent as to put it back in its being; it should consider *that* the essent pre-sents itself and as *what*. But in the interpretation of being as *idea*, not only is an essential consequence twisted into an essence but the falsification is once again misinterpreted. And this too occurred in the course of Greek experience and interpretation.

The idea, as the appearance of the essent, came to constitute its what. Thereby the whatness, the "essence," i.e. the concept of essence, also became ambiguous:

a. an essent asserts itself, it has authority, it summons and brings into being whatever pertains to it, including precisely conflict.

b. an essent asserts itself as this and that; it has this what-determinateness.

We have shown briefly how in the course of the change from *physis* to *idea,* the *ti estin* (quiddity, whatness) emerged and the *hoti estin* (quoddity, that-ness) * came to be distinguished from it. We have thus indicated the origin of *essentia* and *existentia.* Here we shall not go into it more closely. (The question is discussed in an unpublished lecture delivered in the summer semester of 1927.)

But as soon as the essence of being resides in whatness (idea), whatness, as *the* being of the essent, becomes that which is most beingful in an essent. It becomes the actual essent, *ontōs on.* Being as *idea* is exalted, it becomes true being, while being itself, previously dominant, is degraded to what Plato calls *mē on,* what really should not be and really *is* not, because in the realization it always deforms the idea, the pure appearance, by incorporating it in matter. The *idea* now becomes a *paradeigma,* a model. At the same time, the idea necessarily becomes an ideal. The copy actually "is" not; it merely partakes of being, it is a *methexis.* The *chōrismos,* the cleft, has opened between the idea as what really is, the prototype and archetype, and what actually is not, the copy and image.

From the standpoint of the idea, appearing now takes on a new meaning. What appears—the phenomenon—is no longer *physis,* the emerging power, nor is it the self-manifestation of the appearance; no, appearing is now the emergence of the copy. Since the copy never equals its prototype, what appears is *mere* appearance, actually an illusion, a deficiency. Now the *on* becomes distinct from the *phainomenon.* And this development brings with it still another vital consequence. Because the actual repository of being is the *idea* and this is the prototype, all disclosure of being must aim at assimilation to the model, accommodation to idea. The truth of *physis, alē-*

* The fact that something is. R.M.

theia as the unconcealment that is the essence of the emerging power, now becomes *homoiōsis* and *mimēsis*, assimilation and accommodation, orientation by . . . , it becomes a correctness of vision, of apprehension as representation.

Once we fully understand all this, it becomes undeniable that the interpretation of being as *idea* is a far cry from the original beginning. Yet when we speak of a decline it should be noted that this decline remains lofty; it does not sink into baseness. We can judge this loftiness from the following. The great period of Greek being-there was essentially the only classical age; it was so great that it provided the metaphysical conditions underlying the possibility of all classicism. The basic concepts *idea, paradeigma, homoiōsis,* and *mimēsis* foreshadow the metaphysics of classicism. Plato was not yet a classicist, because he could not be one, but he was the classic of classicism. In itself the transformation of being from *physis* to *idea* gave rise to one of the essential movements in the history of the West, and not only of its art.

Now let us see what becomes of the logos with the new interpretation of *physis*. The essent is disclosed in the logos as gathering. This is first effected in language. Consequently the logos becomes the essential determinant of discourse. Language—what is uttered and said and can be said again—is the custodian of the disclosed essent. What has once been said can be repeated and passed on. The truth preserved in it spreads, and in the process the essent originally gathered and disclosed is not each time experienced for itself. In the transmission the truth detaches itself as it were from the essent. This can go so far that the repetition becomes a mere babbling by rote, a *glōssa*. Statement is always exposed to this danger. (See *Sein und Zeit*, § 44b.)

From this it follows that the decision regarding the truth is effected in conflict between authentic discourse and mere babbling. Logos in the sense of discourse and utterance becomes the realm and the scene of decision concerning the truth, i.e. originally, the unconcealment of the essent and hence its being. Initially the logos as gathering *is* the event of unconcealment, grounded in unconcealment and serving it. Now logos as statement becomes the abode of truth in the sense of correctness. And this process culminates in Aristotle's proposition to the effect that logos as statement is that which can be true or false. Truth that was originally unconcealment, a happening of the dominant essent itself, governed by gathering, now becomes an attribute of the logos. In becoming an attribute of statement, the truth not only shifts its abode; it changes its essence as well. From the standpoint of statement, the truth is achieved if discourse adheres to what it speaks of; if the statement follows the essent. The truth becomes the correctness of the logos. With this the logos has departed from its original inclusion in the happening of unconcealment, so that the decision concerning the truth and hence concerning the essent is made on the basis of, and with a view to, the logos; and this applies to the decision not only concerning the essent but even and above all concerning being. Logos is now *legein ti kata tinos*, to say something about something. What is spoken of is what in every case underlies the *statement*, what is set before it ready made ⟨ das ihm Vorliegende ⟩, *hypokeimenon* (*subjectum*). From the standpoint of the logos as independent statement, being becomes *this* being-set-before. (This definition of being, like the *idea*, is foreshadowed in the *physis*. Only the power that emerges of itself can, as presence, come to define itself as appearance and ready-made subject ⟨ Vorliegen ⟩.)

In statement the underlying essent may be represented in different ways: as having such and such properties, such and such magnitude, such and such relations. Properties, magnitude, relations are determinations of being. Because, as modes of being-said, they are derived from logos—and because to state is *kategorein*—the determinations of the being of the essent are called *kategoriai*, categories. Thus the doctrine of being and of the determinations of the essent as such becomes a discipline which searches for the categories and their order. The goal of all ontology is a doctrine of categories. It has long been taken for granted that the essential characteristics of being are categories. But fundamentally it is strange and becomes comprehensible only if we understand not only how the logos as statement broke away from *physis* but how it set itself up in opposition to *physis* as *the* decisive domain, the source of all determinations of being.

But logos, *phasis*, speech in the sense of statement, has become the arbiter over the being of the essent in so profound a sense that whenever one statement stands *against* another, when a contradiction, *antiphasis*, occurs, the contradictory cannot *be*. Conversely, what is not contradictory has at least the possibility of being. The old controversy as to whether Aristotle's principle of contradiction was meant "ontologically" or "logically" is wrongly put, because for Aristotle there was neither "ontology" nor "logic." Both arose only on the basis of Aristotelian philosophy. Actually the principle of contradiction has "ontological" significance because it is a basic law of the logos, a "logical proposition." Accordingly, the suspension of the principle of contradiction in Hegel's dialectic is not an end to the domination of the logos but only its extreme intensification. (That Hegel should have given the name of "logic" to what is actually metaphysics, i.e. "physics," recalls both logos as abode of the categories and logos in the sense of the original *physis*.)

In the form of statement logos itself became something already-there. It became something handy that one handles in order to gain and secure the truth as correctness. The next, short step was to take this method of acquiring truth as a tool, *organon*, that had to be handled in the right way. What made this all the more necessary was that with the change of *physis* to *eidos* and of *logos* to *katēgoria* the *original* disclosure of the being of the essent ceased, and henceforth the true, now interpreted as the correct, merely spread by way of discussion, teaching, and rules, becoming steadily broader and flatter. For the benefit of this process the logos had to be fashioned into a tool. Logic was about to be born.

It was not by mistake that the ancient philosophy of the schools subsumed all the treatises of Aristotle relating to the logos under the title of "Organon." With them logic, in its essentials, was completed. Two thousand years later Kant declared in the preface to the second edition of the *Critique of Pure Reason* that logic "since Aristotle has not taken a single step backward," but "that it has also been unable to take a single step forward to this day and thus to all appearances seems to be concluded and complete." This not only seems to be so. It is so. For despite Kant and Hegel, logic has not made a single advance in the essential and initial questions. The only possible step that remains is to stand on the very ground from which logic rose and to overturn it (as the dominant perspective for the interpretation of being).

Let us now sum up what has been said of *physis* and of *logos: logos* becomes *idea* (*paradeigma*), truth becomes correctness. Logos becomes statement, the locus of truth as correctness, the source of the categories, the fundamental principle in regard to the possibilities of being. "Idea" and "category" become the two terms that dominate Western thought, action, and evaluation, indeed all Western being-there. The transformation of *physis* and *logos* and hence of their relation to one another is a decline from the first beginning. The philosophy of the Greeks conquered the Western world not in its original beginning but in the incipient end, which in Hegel assumed great and definitive form. Where history is authentic it does not die by merely ceasing; it does not just stop living ⟨ver-enden⟩ like the animals; it can only die *historically*.

But what happened, what must have happened to bring Greek philosophy to this incipient end, to this transformation of *physis* and *logos?* This takes us to the second question.

Ad 2. In the change we have described, two factors must be noted.

a. It begins in the very essence of *physis* and *logos*, or more precisely, in a consequence of this essence: what appears (in its shining forth, its seeming) shows an aspect; what has been said enters forthwith into the realm of talk and statement. Thus the change does not come from outside but from "within." But what does "within" mean here? The question does not reside in *physis* for itself and *logos* for itself. We see from Parmenides that the two are essentially connected. The relation between them is the sustaining and governing ground of their essence, "their heart and core," even though the ground of the relation itself is primarily and actually contained in the essence of *physis*. But what is the nature of this relation? This we shall see by stressing a second factor in the change under discussion.

b. In each case a consequence of the change is that, from the standpoint both of the idea and of statement, the original essence of truth, *alētheia* (unconcealment) has changed to correctness. For unconcealment is that heart and core, i.e. the dominant relation between *physis* and *logos* in the original sense. The very essence of dominance is emerging-into-unconcealment. But apprehension and gathering govern the opening up of unconcealment for the essent. The transformation of *physis* and *logos* into idea and statement has its inner ground in a transformation of the essence of truth from unconcealment to correctness.

This essence of truth could not be maintained in its initial, original force. Unconcealment, the space created for the appearing of the essent, broke down. "Idea" and "statement," *ousia* and *katēgoria* were saved from the ruins. When neither the essent nor gathering could be preserved and understood from the standpoint of unconcealment, only *one* possibility remained: the disjoined parts that were already there could only be brought together in a relationship which itself had a character of already-thereness. A ready-made logos had to assimilate and accommodate itself to a ready-made essent as its object. Yet a last glimmer and semblance of the original essence of *alētheia* was preserved. (The already-there necessarily comes forward into unconcealment, and just as necessarily the statement that re-presents ⟨ vor-stellt ⟩ it advances into the same unconcealment.) But the remaining semblance of *alētheia* no longer has sufficient sustaining power or tension to be the determining ground for the essence of truth. And this it has never again become. On the contrary. Ever since idea and category became sovereign, philosophers have tormented themselves in vain, seeking by every possible and impossible stratagem to explain the relation between statement (thinking) and being—in vain, because they never again carried the question of being back to its native ground and soil, thence to unfold it.

Yet the breakdown of unconcealment, as we briefly call this event, did not spring from a mere deficiency, an inability to sustain this essence that was entrusted to historical man. The cause of the breakdown lay first of all in the greatness of the beginning and in the essence of the beginning itself.

("Decline" and "breakdown" are negative terms only in a superficial sense.) Since it is a beginning, the beginning must in a sense leave itself behind. (Thus it necessarily conceals itself, but this self-concealment is not nothing.) A beginning can never directly preserve its full momentum; the only possible way to preserve its force is to repeat, to draw once again ⟨wieder-holen⟩ more deeply than ever from its source. And it is only by repetitive thinking ⟨denkende Wieder-holung⟩ that we can deal appropriately with the beginning and the breakdown of the truth. The need ⟨Not⟩ of being and the greatness of its beginning are no object of a merely historical observation, explanation, and evaluation. This does not preclude but rather requires that the historical course of this collapse be as far as possible elucidated. Here in this lecture a single decisive indication must suffice.

We know from Heraclitus and Parmenides that the unconcealment of being is not simply given. Unconcealment occurs only when it is achieved by work: the work of the word in poetry, the work of stone in temple and statue, the work of the word in thought, the work of the *polis* as the historical place in which all this is grounded and preserved. (In accordance with what has been said above, "work" is to be taken here in the *Greek* sense of *ergon*, the creation that discloses the truth ⟨in die Unverborgenheit herstellen⟩ of something that is present.) The struggle for the unconcealment of the essent and hence for being itself in the work, this struggle for unconcealment, which even in itself is continuous conflict, is at the same time a combat against concealment, disguise, false appearance.

Appearance, *doxa*, is not something beside being and unconcealment; it belongs to unconcealment. But *doxa* is itself ambiguous. It means the view which something presents of itself and at the same time the view that men have. Being-there defines itself in these views. They are stated and passed on. Thus *doxa* is a kind of logos. The prevailing views now block men's view of the essent. The essent is deprived of the possibility of appearing spontaneously and turning *toward* apprehension. The view ⟨Aussicht⟩ that usually turns toward us is distorted into an opinion ⟨Ansicht⟩. The rule of opinions perverts and distorts the essent.

The Greek for "to distort something" is *pseudesthai*. Thus the struggle *for* the unconcealment of the essent, *alētheia*, became a struggle *against pseudos*, distortion and perversion. But it is in the very nature of struggle that whether a contestant wins or loses he becomes dependent on his adversary. Because the battle against untruth is a battle against the *pseudos*, the battle for the truth becomes—from the standpoint of the combated *pseudos*—a battle for the *a-pseudes*, the undistorted, unperverted.

With this the original experience of truth as unconcealment is endangered. For the undistorted is only achieved if apprehension and comprehension are turned, without distortion, straight toward the essent, but this means that they are directed ⟨ sich richten ⟩ by it. The way to truth as correctness ⟨ Richtigkeit ⟩ lies open.

This transformation of unconcealment by way of distortion to undistortion and thence to correctness must be seen in one with the transformation of *physis* to *idea*, of *logos* as gathering to *logos* as statement. On the basis of all this, the definitive interpretation of being that is fixated in the word *ousia* now disengages itself and comes to the fore. It signifies being in the sense of permanent presence, already-thereness. What actually has being is accordingly what always is, *aei on*. Permanently present is what we must go back to in comprehending and producing: the model, the *idea*. Permanently present is what we must go back to in all *logos*, statement; it is what lies-before, *hypokeimenon*, *subjectum*. From the standpoint of *physis*, emergence, what was always-there is the *proteron*, the earlier, the a priori.

This determination of the being of the essent comes to characterize all comprehension and statement of the essent. The *hypokeimenon* is the forerunner of the subsequent interpretation of the essent as object. Apprehension, *noein*, is taken over by the logos in the sense of statement. Thus it becomes the apprehension which, in determining something as something, thinks-through ⟨ durch-nimmt, durch-vernimmit ⟩ what it encounters, *dianoeisthai*. This discursive thinking-through defines the understanding in the sense of evaluating representation. Apprehension becomes understanding; apprehension becomes reason.

Christianity reinterprets the being of the essent as created being. Thought and knowledge come to be differentiated from faith (*fides*). This does not impede the rise of rationalism and irrationalism but rather prepares the way for it and intensifies it.

The essent is held to have been created by God, i.e. rationally preconceived. Hence as soon as the creature's relation to the creator is relaxed and, concomitantly, as man's reason makes itself predominant and even sets itself up as absolute, the being of the essent inevitably becomes thinkable in terms of pure mathematical thought. This calculable and calculated being makes the essent into what can be mastered by modern, mathematically structured technology, which is something *essentially* different from every other hitherto known use of tools.

Essent is only what, when correctly thought, stands up to correct thinking.

The principal name, i.e. the crucial interpretation of the being of the essent is *ousia*. As a philosophical concept the word means permanent presence. At the time when this word had already become a name for the dominant concept of philosophy, it still retained its original meaning: *hē hyperchousa ousia* (Isocrates) signifies present property status. But even this basic meaning of *ousia* with its implications for the interpretation of being could not maintain itself. *Ousia* now began to be interpreted as *substantia*. This meaning retained its currency in the Middle Ages and in the modern era down to our own day. And Greek philosophy has been interpreted retroactively, i.e. falsified from top to bottom from the standpoint of the dominant concept of substance—the concept of function is only its mathematical variant.

Thus *ousia* has become the decisive term for being. It still remains to be seen how the distinctions between being and becoming, being and appearance, are conceived in the light of this *ousia*. We recall the schema of our distinctions:

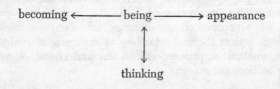

becoming ←——————— being ———————→ appearance

↑
↓

thinking

In opposition to becoming stands eternal permanence. In opposition to appearance as mere semblance stands what is actually seen, the *idea* which, as the *ontōs on*, is again the permanent and enduring as opposed to changing appearance. But becoming and appearance are not determined only on the basis of *ousia*, for *ousia* in turn has been essentially defined by its relation to logos, discursive judgment, *dianoia*. Accordingly, becoming and appearance are defined in the perspective of thought.

From the standpoint of evaluating thought, which always starts from something permanent, becoming appears as impermanence. In the realm of the already-there, impermanence is manifested primarily as not remaining in the same place. Becoming is seen as change of place, *phora*, transposition. All becoming is regarded as motion, and the decisive aspect of motion is change of place. With the rising domination of thought in the sense of modern mathematical rationalism no other form of becoming besides motion as change of place is recognized. Where other phenomena of motion show themselves, one tries to understand them in terms of change of place. Change of place itself, motion, is in turn conceived in terms of velocity: $v = \dfrac{s}{t}$. In his Regulae (No. xii) Descartes, the philosophical founder of this mode of thought, ridiculed every other concept of motion.

Like becoming, appearance, the other antithesis to being, is also determined in accordance with *ousia*, from the standpoint of thought (calculation). Appearance, illusion, is the incorrect. Its ground is to be sought in distorted thinking. Appearance becomes mere logical incorrectness, fallacy. Now for the first time we can measure the full bearing of the opposition between thought and being: thought establishes its domination (in respect to the crucial determination of essence) over being and at the same time over what is opposed to being. This domination goes still further. For as soon as logos in the sense of statement assumes the rule over being, the moment being is experienced and conceived as *ousia*, already-thereness, the distinction between being and the ought is in preparation. Our schema of the delimitations of being now looks as follows:

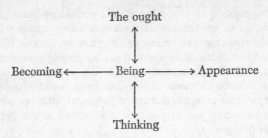

4. Being and the Ought

As our diagram suggests, this distinction goes in another direction. The distinction between being and thinking is downward. This indicates that thought is the sustaining and determining ground of being. The differentiation between being and the ought, on the other hand, is upward. This suggests that while being is grounded in thought it is surmounted by the ought. In other words: being is no longer the decisive factor. But is it not after all the idea, the prototype? Yes, but precisely because of their character as prototypes, ideas are no longer decisive. For since the idea presents a view ⟨ Aussehen ⟩, it is in a sense an essent (*on*), and as such demands in turn a determination of *its* being, i.e. once again a single view. According to Plato the idea of ideas, the supreme idea, is the *idea tou agathou,* the idea of the good.

Here the "good" does not mean the morally proper but the valiant ⟨ das Wackere ⟩, which accomplishes and can accomplish what is appropriate. The *agathon* is the standard as such, what first endows being with the power ⟨ Vermögen ⟩ to become a prototype. The bestower of such power is the first potency. But insofar as the ideas constitute being, *ousia,* the *idea tou agathou,* the supreme idea, stands *epekeina tēs ousias,* beyond being. Thus being itself, not as such but *as idea,* comes into opposition to something other, on which it, being, is dependent. The supreme idea has become the model of the models.

No elaborate discussions are now needed to show that in this differentiation, as in the others, what is set apart from

being, the ought, is not superimposed on being from somewhere outside. Being itself, interpreted as idea, brings with
it a relation to the prototypical, the exemplary, the ought. As
being itself becomes fixated as idea, it strives to make good
the resulting degradation of being. But by now this is possible
only if something is set *above* being, something that being
never is yet but always *ought* to be.

Here we have wished only to elucidate the essential origin
of the distinction between being and the ought or what is
basically the same, its historical beginning. We shall not go
into the history of its developments and transformations. We
wish to make only *one* essential point. In connection with all
the determinations of being and the distinctions we have mentioned, we must bear one thing in mind: because being is
initially *physis*, the power that emerges and discloses, it discloses itself as *eidos* and *idea*. This interpretation never rests
exclusively or even primarily on philosophical exegesis.

We have seen that the ought is opposed to being as soon
as being defines itself as idea. With this definition, thought
as the logos of statement (*dialegesthai*) assumes a crucial role.
Thus it is in the modern era, when this very same thought
becomes dominant in the form of self-sufficient reason, that
the distinction between being and the ought really comes
into its own. The process is completed in Kant. For Kant the
essent is nature, i.e. that which can be determined and is determined in mathematical-physical thinking. To nature is opposed the categorical imperative, also determined by reason
and as reason. In relating it to the mere essent as instinctive
nature Kant calls it explicitly the ought ⟨Sollen⟩. Fichte
proceeded to make the opposition between being and the
ought the express foundation of his system. In the course of
the nineteenth century the priority passed to the essent in the
Kantian sense—the empirical world of the sciences which now
took in the historical and economic sciences. This predomi-
nance of the essent endangered the ought in its role as standard
and criterion. The ought was compelled to bolster up its claim
by seeking its ground in itself. The moral claim ⟨Sollensan-
spruch⟩ had to present its own justification. Obligation, the
ought, could emanate only from something which in itself
raised a moral claim, which had an intrinsic *value*, which was

itself a *value*. The values as such now became the foundation
of morality (the ought). But since the values are opposed to
the being of the essent in the sense of facts, they themselves
cannot *be*. Therefore they were said to have validity. The values became the crucial criteria for all realms of the essent, i.e.
of the already-there. History came to be regarded as a realization of values.

Plato conceived being as idea. The idea was a prototype
and as such set the measure. What seems more plausible than
to take Plato's ideas in the sense of values and to interpret
the being of the essent from the standpoint of value?

The values have validity. But validity is still too suggestive
of what is valid for a subject. Exalted as value, the ought was
again in need of bolstering up. To this end a being was attributed to the values themselves. *At bottom* this being meant
neither more nor less than the presence of something already-
there, though not in so vulgar and handy a sense as chairs
and tables. With the being of values a maximum of confusion
and uprootedness was achieved. Since the term "value" was
gradually beginning to look worn, particularly as it also played
a part in economic theory, the values were now called "totalities" ⟨ Ganzheiten ⟩. But with this term only the letters had
changed, though it is true that to call them totalities brings
out their true character as halves, inadequacies ⟨ Halbheiten ⟩.
But in essential matters halves are more disastrous than the
so dreaded nothingness. In 1928 there appeared the first part
of a general bibliography on the concept of value. In it 661
titles are listed. No doubt the number has meanwhile swollen
to one thousand. All these works call themselves philosophy.
The works that are being peddled about nowadays as the philosophy of National Socialism but have nothing whatever to
do with the inner truth and greatness of this movement
(namely the encounter between global technology and modern man)—have all been written by men fishing in the trou-
bled waters of "values" and "totalities."

How stubbornly the idea of values ingrained itself in the
nineteenth century can be seen from the fact that even Nietzsche, and precisely he, never departed from this perspective.
The subtitle of his projected magnum opus, "The Will to
Power," is "An Attempt to Re-evaluate All Values." The third

book is called: "An Attempt to Establish New Values." His entanglement in the thicket of the idea of values, his failure to understand its questionable origin, is the reason why Nietzsche did not attain to the true center of philosophy. Even if a future philosopher should reach this center—we of the present day can only work toward it—he will not escape entanglement, but it will be a different entanglement. No one can jump over his own shadow.

We have inquired our way through the four distinctions: being and becoming, being and appearance, being and thinking, being and the ought. At the beginning of our discussion we listed seven points by way of orientation. At first it seemed as though we were engaged in a mere exercise of thought, a differentiation between terms arbitrarily thrown together.

We shall now repeat them in the same form and ask ourselves: has the discussion maintained the direction indicated in these points and has it achieved the insight we were seeking?

1. In these distinctions being is delimited from something else and therefore, *in* this delimitation, already has determinateness.

2. It is delimited in four interrelated respects. Therefore the determinateness of being must become ramified and increase accordingly.

3. These distinctions are by no means accidental. What is held apart in them belonged originally together and tends to merge. The distinctions therefore have an inner necessity.

4. Consequently the oppositions, which look at first sight like formulas, did not arise fortuitously and find their way into the language as figures of speech. They arose in close connection with the crucial Western form of being. They began with the beginning of philosophical questioning.

5. Not only have these distinctions remained dominant in Western philosophy. They permeate all knowledge, action, and discourse even when they are not specifically mentioned or not in these words.

6. The order in which the titles have been listed provides

in itself an indication of the order of their essential context
and of the historical order in which they were moulded.

7. If one is to *ask* the question of being radically, one must
understand the task of unfolding the true essence of *being;*
one must come to a decision regarding the powers hidden in
these distinctions, in order to bring them back to their own
truth.

Everything asserted in these points has now been brought
to view, with the exception of the last point. It alone contains
a demand. In conclusion we wish to show that it is justified
and that its fulfillment is necessary.

To carry out this demonstration we must cast one more
glance over the whole of this "Introduction to Metaphysics."

Everything depends on the fundamental question stated at
the beginning: "Why are there essents rather than nothing?"
In order to develop this fundamental question we were compelled to ask a preliminary question: "How does it stand with
being?"

At first "being" struck us as an empty word, its meaning a
vapor. This seemed to be a demonstrable fact among others.
But in the end what was seemingly unquestionable and sus-
ceptible of no further inquiry proved to be *the worthiest of
all questions.* Being and the understanding of being are not a
given fact. Being is the basic happening which first makes possible historical being-there amid the disclosure of the essent
as a whole.

But we can experience this worthiest and most problematic
ground of historical being-there in its dignity and rank only
if we question it. Accordingly, we asked the preliminary question: "How does it stand with being?"

A look at the familiar but diversified usage of the "is" con-
vinced us that it is a mistake to talk about the indeterminateness and emptiness of being. The "is" determines the meaning
and content of the infinitive "sein" ⟨ being ⟩, and not the other
way around. We are now in a position to see *why* this must
be so. In statement the "is" serves as a copula, as a "little
word of relation" (Kant). But because statement, *logos* as
katēgoria, has become a court of judgment over being, *it* defines being on the basis of *its own* "is," the "is" of statement.
The being which we took at the start as an empty word

must therefore, contrary to this appearance, have a determinate meaning.

The determinateness of being was shown by the discussion of the four distinctions.

Over against becoming being is permanence.

Over against appearance being is the enduring prototype, the always identical.

Over against thought it is the underlying, the already-there.

Over against the ought it is the datum, the ought that is not yet realized or already realized.

Permanent, always identical, already-there, given—all mean fundamentally the same: enduring presence, *on* as *ousia*.

This definition of being is not accidental. It has grown out of the determination which dominates our historical being-there by virtue of its great beginning among the Greeks. If being has determinateness it is not because we have delimited a mere word meaning. The determinateness of being is *the* power which still sustains and dominates all our relations to the essent as a whole, to becoming, to appearance, to thinking, and to the ought.

The question of how it stands with being proves to be the question of how it stands with our being-there in history, the question of whether we *stand* in history or merely stagger. From a metaphysical point of view, we *are staggering*. We move about in all directions amid the essent, and no longer know how it stands with being. Least of all do we know that we no longer know. We stagger even when we assure one another that we are no longer staggering, even when, as in recent years, people do their best to show that this inquiry about being brings only confusion, that its effect is destructive, that it is nihilism. [One must be very naïve to suppose that this misinterpretation of the question about being, renewed since the appearance of existentialism, is new.]

But where is nihilism really at work? Where men cling to familiar essents and suppose that it suffices to go on taking essents as essents, since after all that is what they are. But with this they reject the question of being and treat being like a nothing (*nihil*) which in a certain sense it is, insofar as it has an essence. To forget being and cultivate only the essent —that is nihilism. Nihilism thus understood is the *ground of* the nihilism which Nietzsche exposed in the first book of *The Will to Power*.

By *contrast*, to press inquiry into being explicitly to the limits of nothingness, to draw nothingness into the question of being—this is the first and only fruitful step toward a true transcending of nihilism.

The discussion of the four distinctions shows us precisely that the inquiry into being as that which is most problematic of all must be carried this far. Being is delimited *over against* becoming, appearance, thought, the ought—these are not something that has just been dreamed up. They represent powers that dominate and bewitch the essent, its disclosure and configuration, its closing and disfigurement. Becoming—is it nothing? Appearance—is it nothing? Thought—is it nothing? The ought—is it nothing? By no means.

But if all that is opposed to being in the distinctions is *not* nothing, then it is *essent* and ultimately more so than what is regarded as essent in the restricted, current view of being. But in what sense of being *are* becoming and appearing, are thinking and the ought *essent*? Certainly not in *the* sense of the being from which they are distinguished. But this sense of being has been the current one ever since antiquity.

Then the sense of being that has been accepted up until now does not suffice to name everything that "is."

For this reason being must be experienced anew from the bottom up and in all the breadth of its possible essence if we are to set our historical being-there to work in a historical way. For the powers that oppose being, the differentiations themselves, have long determined and dominated our being-there; complexly intertwined, they have long beset our being-there and held it in confusion with regard to "being." Thus a fundamental inquiry into the four distinctions shows that the being which they encircle must itself be transformed into the encircling circle and ground of all the essent. The *one* basic differentiation, whose intensity and fundamental cleavage sustain history, is the differentiation between being and the essent.

But how is this differentiation to be made? Where can philosophy begin to think it? Yet here we should not speak of a beginning but re-enact it; for it *is* accomplished, it was accomplished in the necessity of the beginning under which we still stand. It is not for nothing that in discussing the four distinctions we dwelt at disproportionate length on the distinction between being and thinking. Today it is still the sustaining ground, the basis on which being is determined. Thought guided by *logos* as statement has supplied and maintained the perspective in which being is seen.

Thus if being itself is to be disclosed and grounded in *its* original differentiation from the essent, an original perspective must be opened. The beginnings of the differentiation between being and thinking, the divergence between apprehension and being, make it clear that what is at stake is nothing less than a humanity, a being-human determined by the essence of being (*physis*), that we are trying to open up.

The question of who man is is closely bound up with the question of the essence of being. But the definition of the essence of man required here cannot be the product of an arbitrary anthropology that considers man in basically the same way as zoology considers animals. Here the direction and scope of the question of being-human are determined *solely* through the question of *being*. In accordance with the hidden message of the beginning, man should be understood, within the question of being, as *the* site which being requires in order to disclose itself. Man is the site of openness, the there. The essent juts into this there and is fulfilled. Hence we say that man's being is in the strict sense of the word "being-there." The perspective for the opening of being must be grounded originally in the essence of being-there as such a site for the disclosure of being.

The whole Western view of being, the whole tradition and accordingly the relation to being that still prevails, are summed up in the heading "being and thought."

But being and time ⟨ Sein und Zeit ⟩ is a title that cannot in any way be equated with the differentiations we have been discussing. It points in an entirely different direction of inquiry.

Here the "word" time is not merely substituted for the "word" thought; rather, the essence of time, wholly within the area of the question of being, is fundamentally determined in other respects.

But why time? Because in the beginning of Western philosophy the *perspective governing* the disclosure of being was time, though this perspective *as such* remained hidden—and inevitably so. When ultimately *ousia,* meaning permanent presence, became the basic concept of time, what was the unconcealed foundation of permanence and presence if not time? But *this* "time" remained essentially undeveloped and (on the basis and in the perspective of "physics") could not be developed. For as soon as reflection on the essence of time began, at the *end* of Greek philosophy with Aristotle, time itself had to be taken as something somehow present, *ousia tis.* Consequently time was considered from the standpoint of the "now," the actual moment. The past is the "no-*longer*-now," the future is the "not-*yet*-now." Being in the sense of already-thereness (presence) became the perspective for the determination of time. But time was not the perspective specially chosen for the interpretation of being.

In such a reflection I am not referring to my book *Sein und Zeit* but to a problem. The true problem is what we do not know and what, insofar as we know it *authentically,* namely *as* a problem, we know only *questioningly.*

To know how to question means to know how to wait, even a whole lifetime. But an age which regards as real only what goes fast and can be clutched with both hands looks on questioning as "remote from reality" and as something that does not pay, whose benefits cannot be numbered. But the essential is not number; the essential is the right time, i.e. the right moment, and the right perseverance.

"For," as Hölderlin said, "the mindful God abhors untimely growth." ("Aus dem Motivkreis der Titanen," *Sämtliche Werke, 4,* 218.)

INDEX